ARIZONA WILDFLOWERS

Book Designer: MARY WINKELMAN VELGOS

Photography Editor: PETER ENSENBERGER

Production: KIM ENSENBERGER, VICKY SNOW

Map Designer: ROBERT W. TOPE

Botanical Illustrator: PAUL R. MARTIN

Technical Editors: PAUL R. MARTIN, SUSAN EUBANK

Copy Editors: PK PERKIN MCMAHON, BOB ALBANO

Book Editor: EVELYN HOWELL

Printing History
1988 — Originally published by *Arizona Highways* as *Desert Wildflowers: A Guide for Identifying, Locating, and Enjoying Arizona Wildflowers and Cactus Blossoms.* Original text and technical editing by Desert Botanical Garden staff, including Gary Paul Nabhan, Assistant Director; Mary Irish, Director of Public Horticulture; and Jane Cole, Garden Librarian. Original illustrations and maps by James R. Metcalf.
1997 — Updated for second edition. Additional maps by Kevin Kibsey.
2006 — Expanded , revised, reformatted, and retitled for third edition. Supplemental text by Evelyn Howell.
Printed in Hong Kong.

Published by the Book Division of *Arizona Highways* magazine, a monthly publication of the Arizona Department of Transportation, 2039 West Lewis Avenue, Phoenix, Arizona 85009. Telephone: (602) 712-2200.
Web site: www.arizonahighways.com
Win Holden - Publisher
Bob Albano - Managing Editor
Evelyn Howell - Associate Editor
PK Perkin McMahon - Associate Editor
Peter Ensenberger - Director of Photography
Kim Ensenberger - Production Director

Library of Congress Catalog Number 2004104397
ISBN 1-932082-27-1

FRONT COVER:
LOOKING DELICATE, SOME SCORPION-WEED UNFURLS AGAINST THE STURDY PADS OF A PRICKLY PEAR CACTUS. Bruce Griffin

BACK COVER
A MOGOLLON RIM MEADOW NEAR CHEVELON CANYON BLOOMS WITH YELLOW CONEFLOWERS, BLUE LARKSPUR, AND PURPLE WILD BERGAMOT. Nick Berezenko

ARIZONA
WILDFLOWERS

A YEAR-ROUND GUIDE TO NATURE'S BLOOMS

Text by
DESERT BOTANICAL GARDEN STAFF and *ARIZONA HIGHWAYS* STAFF

Photographs by
ARIZONA HIGHWAYS CONTRIBUTORS

ARIZONA HIGHWAYS
BOOKS

SCORPION-WEED / Chuck Lawsen

MANY FLOWERED FOUR-O'CLOCK / Larry Ulrich

SACRED DATURA / Bruce Griffin

ROCKY MOUNTAIN BEEPLANT / Larry Ulrich

CONTENTS

PREFACE

The winter wildflower displays across Arizona's deserts have made the state renowned for rainbow swaths of color. Working with the Desert Botanical Garden in Phoenix, *Arizona Highways* magazine celebrated this rainbow by publishing *Desert Wildflowers* in 1988. That the book has gone back to print four more times speaks of the ongoing fascination with desert wildflowers.

However, Arizona encompasses more than just desert, and those other habitats abound with their own distinct wildflowers — in canyons and mountain meadows, in pine forests and central uplands. We wanted to share the scope of that beauty, too. So when we were readying the wildflowers book for its sixth printing, we chose to expand it.

Now, these pages hold a glimpse of the delicate, petaled art that flourishes across this diverse state, from the border with Mexico to the floor of the Grand Canyon, from the Four Corners region down to the expanse of the Sonoran Desert.

We also updated some scientific names. Depending on which botanical reference is used, quite a degree of variation exists with plant names. For the sake of consistency and universality, this book uses the scientific name recognized by the federal government's Integrated Taxonomic Information System (ITIS); ITIS results from a partnership between U.S. agencies and their counterparts in Canada and Mexico, providing authoritative taxonomic information on plants (as well as animals, fungi, and microbes). If an alternative scientific name (called a synonym) was previously familiar, but is no longer officially accepted, we listed the synonym in brackets. To use ITIS yourself, go to www.itis.usda.gov/ and search by common or scientific name. Common names, of course, can be even more varied in structure and spelling, so when in doubt, we again deferred to the ITIS, except for a few cases where Webster's Collegiate Dictionary had the last word. For local flavor, we included some alternative common names that are known regionally, but that the ITIS missed.

By whatever names we choose to call them, please join us in cherishing Arizona's array of wildflowers.

— *Evelyn Howell*
Book Editor

SCORPION-WEEDS
SURROUND MEXICAN
GOLDPOPPIES AND
TEDDY BEAR CHOLLA.
Jeff Snyder

THE FLORAL CHORUS
Sung in the Wild, Heard in the Heart

We listened hard, for Arizona's wilderness was calling us that April. We could hear it as subtle music beneath the coyote's howl, the burrowing owl's call, and the chiming droplets of desert springs.

The distant choir sang from the Pinta Sand Dunes in the Cabeza Prieta Wildlife Refuge in southwestern Arizona. The spring winds rustled the blazingstars, snowy sunflowers, desert marigolds, and lupines. The ribbony leaves of the ajo lilies sang in the sand as they sketched an arc around their trumpet-like blooms.

With the blossoms beckoning, we went out to meet the music. And yet, as we left our homes in Phoenix, Tucson, and Flagstaff, we had no way of knowing whether the wildflowers still would be showing by the time we reached them. Some stage only a two- to three-week appearance in bloom before they wither. Other summer bloomers sustain only a six- to eight-week lifespan as annual plants. They then leave their seeds or bulbs in the soil, mute until a good rain springs them to life some other year.

Wildflowers, like the stones that naturalist Annie Dillard has described, may or may not talk, let alone sing. And yet, we still gain something by tuning in to them, by listening for their wildness.

When Arizona's wildflowers do call, sometimes they do so with the visible equivalent of a high-decibel shout. On one occassion, at Picacho Peak between Phoenix and Tucson, the goldpoppy show was spectacular enough to keep highway traffic past it slowed to 10 miles an hour. At Kitt Peak you can watch the desert floor below break open into a kaleidoscope of colorful goldpoppies, owl clovers, verbenas, chias, and globemallows. Along Interstate 17, rising north toward New River from Phoenix, the brittlebush and the paloverde trees can paint the volcanic hills a gaudy golden for weeks on end. Outside Flagstaff, Forest Service roads meander past high forest meadows spiked with the rich purple of Rocky Mountain irises.

Arizona's wildflower hunters have developed into an opportunistic breed, ready to roam at the hint of a floral show. I know several plant fanatics who will drive a hundred miles out of their way for a chance to lie down amidst a mixed stand of "bellyflowers" — the assorted wildflowers hugging the earth, so tiny that you must be less than a nose-length away to recognize their microscopic blossoms. Other friends of mine suddenly

WITH THE EAGLE TAIL MOUNTAINS AGAINST THE HORIZON, DESERT SAND VERBENA ENGULF SOME DUNE EVENING PRIMROSE.
Randy A. Prentice

arrange evening gatherings of viewers when their night-blooming cereus cactus decides to open.

But you don't have to drive a hundred miles, or even 10, to savor the beauty of Arizona's plants. This was brought home to us by an elderly Indian friend of ours, a man who has never owned a car or traveled very far from his Sonoran Desert place of birth.

Every year, our families would visit at Easter time. With cane in hand, he would walk us around his yard, showing us the flowers that had volunteered or self-sown, the others that he had planted, and still others tended by his wife.

My friend's imagination had been captured many years ago by the beardtongue that he called "wind's flower" in his native tongue. The wind, he claimed, blew the seeds into his yard years before. When he saw the plants rise, he watered them and weeded away competitors. The next year, when winter came, they arose again, but from an entirely different spot within his yard. Again he cared for them with the same fervor as if they were prize roses he'd bought from a nursery. The next year, he began to walk his yard earlier in the season, curious to find where they would pop up next.

Soon, he began selecting variants, encouraging whitish and multi-lobed mutants to shed their seeds more abundantly. By the time our friend had gone blind with age, his yard had become a menagerie of the wind's flowers.

And the memory of their beauty still hangs before his mind's eye. The beauty of wildflowers is a kind that you can take with you, but not merely by picking a bundle or by taking snapshots; you can let their colors, shapes, and fragrances seep deeply into your life. This book is in praise of the cactus flower, the gourd blossom, and the tiny blooms of anonymous bellyflowers that make us stop and take notice of the Earth around us.

It also is in praise of the people who have let these other organisms into their daily lives — and to help you do the same.

— Gary Paul Nabhan
    Former Assistant Director, 1986-1992
    Desert Botanical Garden
    Phoenix, Arizona

LIKE A CHORUS OF YELLOW, BRITTLEBUSHES FLOWER ON THE SLOPES OF PICACHO PEAK STATE PARK. Paul Gill

GAMES OF CHANCE
Why Wildflowers Bloom When They Do

The previous October, a hurricane fringe storm had soaked southern Arizona, and now we saw the springtime payoff of those rains. From the flanks of Kitt Peak west of Tucson, on the access road to the National Observatory, we could look out over the valley and see a sunburst of yellow-orange more than a half-mile wide.

In this grand display of goldpoppies that struck us with awe we also sensed an underlying fragility. Had the valley grasses grown heavily the previous fall, their dead stalks would have smothered the emerging poppies. If no rains had followed late October's gully-washer, most of the seedlings would have withered and died. Any number of weather quirks could have scattered or diluted this dramatic concentration of color.

Instead, we saw the simultaneous blooming of hundreds of thousands of goldpoppies, a spellbinder. For reasons not clearly understood, such a spectacle would not appear the following year, or the next.

Beyond the sculpted metropolitan landscapes, where irrigation ensures that exotic ornamentals stay in flower, something wild is in bloom in Arizona year-round. While snow may blanket the vegetation of many states, Arizona sees spring wildflowers breaking into bud at least as early as February. A succession of herbs, trees, and cacti keep flowering up until the summer rainy season, or "monsoons," begin in late June or early July, and then some of those same plants flower again. Others unfold their color through the late summer and fall, and some green plants prolong their blossoming and fruiting if it rains in October or early November. But foretelling exactly where the flowers will unfold and how many, sometimes even predicting when, is a gamble — delightful if you can allow yourself to be surprised, frustrating if you were counting on repeat performances of a favorite mass bloom.

Even in moderately dry years, Decembers may come in colorfully with brittlebush, fairy duster, and desert broom still in bloom. Perhaps we've cheated a little, and the blooming seems continuous because this book's definition of "wildflower" is so generous. In addition to the characteristic low-growing, flowering green plants, the wildflower list here includes certain showy native trees and shrubs, cacti, and succulents, along with a few introduced plants that have made themselves forever at home in Arizona's landscape.

SPIKES OF LUPINE
ACCENT A FIELD OF
MEXICAN
GOLDPOPPIES.
Chuck Lawsen

Those floral world travelers aside, it is Arizona's assortment of native plants that gives the state part of its identity, a distinctive visual signature that contributes to our sense of place. Many of us want to bring a touch of this distinctive environment to our own yards by adding wildflower plantings. We're happy to find nursery stock and seed packets that let us do just that. But then we have to ask, if we can buy these natives commercially, to what extent are they truly wild? Simply put, wildflowers are any plants with showy blooms that have not been hybridized, or genetically bred. Found in the wild or propagated in a nursery, they can be the low-lying trumpet flowers, the millions of sweet pale clusters hanging from a mesquite tree, or the crown of creamy blossoms atop a giant saguaro.

On their own in their natural environment, wildflowers reproduce and endure without human intervention, although many respond well to any extra water or nutrients offered to them. The true test of their wildness comes when we broadcast our backyard-harvested seeds back into a natural, untended environment. If they can be found germinating and successfully reseeding for many years to come, then they have not become as domesticated as our backyard vegetables and houseplants. Exotic ornamentals with the threads of their evolutionary history bred out of them are more apt to fail under the unpredictable conditions that Nature has to offer, especially under Arizona's stressful extremes.

Wildflower seeds may not germinate all at once. By spreading out seedling emergence over several weeks each year, and several years overall, a wildflower population can avoid devastation from a single catastrophic event such as an unseasonable freeze or locust epidemic.

One species may have a longer bloom time than another, but if each of their individuals flowers on a different day, the results are not as spectacular as those species whose plants briefly bloom simultaneously. In fact, mass flowering is more common among short-duration bloomers, such as goldpoppies, than for those which produce a few flowers per day over a long duration, such as sacred daturas or mallows.

Foothills paloverde trees light up the desert when they bloom, but their entire season may run less than three weeks. Rather than exploding in a single burst of white, pink, and purple, desert willow flowers may open and fade, one by one, over a seven-month period, so they seldom change our view of the landscape so dramatically.

For those of us who enjoy this unpredictability, wildflowers satisfy our aesthetics in another way. Within a stand of the same species, not all individuals flower identically. Unlike hybrid agricultural crops, wild plants are not uniform in size, shape, or color. So near Casa Grande in the spring, travelers often notice white lupines sprinkled in among the true blue ones.

With such genetic variation, matched to the vagaries of the desert environment, wild plants adapt their flowering patterns: They can flower

A SAGUARO'S CLUSTER OF BUDS BEGINS TO FLOWER. Jack Dykinga

YELLOW BRITLEBUSH FLOWERS (RIGHT) ENTWINE WITH A FULL SPREAD OF HEDGEHOG CACTUS FLOWERS. Paul Gill

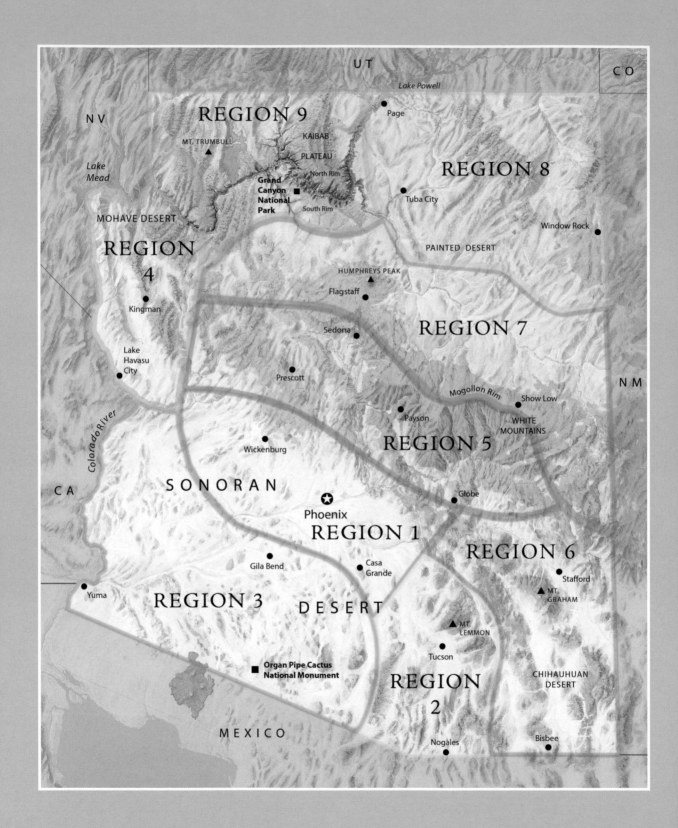

REGION 9

REGION 8

REGION 4

REGION 7

REGION 5

REGION 1

REGION 6

REGION 3

REGION 2

UT

CO

NV

CA

NM

MEXICO

Lake Powell

Page

MT. TRUMBULL

KAIBAB
PLATEAU

North Rim

Lake
Mead

Grand
Canyon
National
Park

South Rim

Tuba City

Window Rock

MOHAVE DESERT

PAINTED DESERT

HUMPHREYS PEAK

Flagstaff

Kingman

Sedona

Lake
Havasu
City

Colorado River

Prescott

Mogollon Rim

Show Low

Payson

WHITE
MOUNTAINS

Wickenburg

SONORAN

Phoenix

Globe

Gila Bend

Casa
Grande

Stafford

MT.
GRAHAM

Yuma

DESERT

MT.
LEMMON

Tucson

CHIHAUHUAN
DESERT

Organ Pipe Cactus
National Monument

Nogales

Bisbee

in a drought year when having grown no higher than your hand span, but give them a wet year, and they will stretch and bloom at waist height. Their size, shape, and maturation all flex to meet impending challenges.

Here, where rainfall can vary fourfold from best to worst years in the same decade, annual wildflower heights can vary 16-fold. Inundated by runoff, an island within a desert arroyo may have 20 times the plant growth of adjacent rocky slopes. And a low-lying basin receiving a heavier frost may see its flowering season shrink, while a butte nearby escapes the freeze to dazzle all beholders.

Keep in mind that there is not just one Arizona desert, and that Arizona is not all desert, but a patchwork of alpine forest, evergreen woodlands, isolated wetlands, semiarid grasslands, and mountain meadows. Mountains tower suddenly from the desert floor, and plateaus drop suddenly into secret canyons. The dominant vegetation of any place is shaped by elevation and terrain, extreme high and low temperatures, frequency of freezes or fires, seasonality of rainfall, and duration of drought. These factors also affect which companion populations of annuals and small cacti grow and flower beneath the tree and shrub canopies.

The regions marked across the state map in this book try to account for some of these variables, but no single region is topographically or climatically uniform. The imaginary boundaries imposed here try to parallel certain vegetation/climate combinations, like the Sonoran Desert, and physical features that change the face of the terrain, like the Mogollon Rim on Region 5's border with Region 7. Region 2 encompasses Tucson's saguaro cactus stands and Mt. Lemmon's forested slopes, peaking at 9,157 feet — a summit that in some winters sees enough snowfall to ski on. Region 9 encompasses Grand Canyon National Park, even though the Canyon's North Rim, about 1,500 feet higher than the South Rim, is cooler and wetter — and points along the Canyon's floor, like Phantom Ranch, may match distant Phoenix more than the nearby Kaibab Plateau. Despite this dramatic array of differences across the Grand Canyon region, a plant species may grow on both Rims and down in the Canyon, coordinating its flowering timetable with each locale's growing season. In this southwestern state, variation is the rule.

Arizona is not all desert, but it is arid. When a habitat is referred to as "wetter," the term is relative to other parts of the state; don't expect that habitat to display copious moisture, because the difference in annual precipitation, from desert to mountain forest, may be less than 2 inches overall.

Different sets of wildflowers "read" these dry conditions in distinctive ways. Drought escapers grow only when conditions are mild and moist. Yet they will grow so rapidly that they can mature in six to 12 weeks. Before drought has a chance to set in again, they have bloomed, fruited, and gone dormant or died; they have escaped a dry, harsh time of the year.

Some longer-lived plants outlast the drier times by drawing upon water reserves not available to the flowering annuals. The mesquite tree often roots along floodplains to reach into the underground flow of soil moisture. When growing along permanent streams, however low they may run, mesquites never truly experience water stress. Also found in uplands or away from rivers, mature mesquites often grow roots extending more than 30 feet deep, and some mesquite roots have reached as far down as 150 feet! Their large root area extends beyond the scarcity to absorb adequate water and nutrients.

Cacti, agaves, and other succulents, such as tuberous wild gourd plants, draw upon water stored in their own tissue. During dry periods, they close up shop, slough off their tiny root hairs, and minimize water loss. Within 24 hours of a drenching rain, their roots are reactivated, and root hairs grow back in the upper layers of the soil to quickly absorb surface soil moisture. Their tissues swell with water to tide them over the subsequent months. A barrel cactus can continue growth without any replenishment of its water stores for a month and a half after the soil becomes drier than the plant.

Some trees and shrubs drop their leaves during drought to minimize water loss, but they still carry on some food-making activities via their photosynthetic bark. Drought tolerators like this include paloverde trees

THIS LOCATION IN THE SUPERSTITION MOUNTAINS, SHOT ON MARCH 24, 1999, SHOWS A SLOPE TOO DRY TO BLOOM. Paul Gill

and ocotillos. Other trees and shrubs do not have massive stores of water to fall back on — the true drought resisters, they must bear the brunt of harsh conditions. They have only tiny leaves to begin with, which often are covered with resins or tiny gray hairs to reduce heat loading and water loss. Drought resisters like the creosote bush drop their leaves only under the most extreme water deficits but re-leaf rapidly once rain comes again.

Wild plants do more than just survive. They interact with their animal pollinators, a relationship reflected in their flower size, color, scent, and timing.

Each pollinator has special nutritional needs that are met by the kinds of sugars and other nutrients in the flowers it visits. A short bloom period may indicate dependency upon a particular migrating bird, bat, or insect pollinator, without which these plants produce fewer fertile seeds. A woody species that has all of its individuals blooming simultaneously more easily catches a pollinator's notice. Hummingbirds tend to favor long, tubular flowers that are red, purple, orange, or pink and that offer sucrose-rich nectars. Bats specialize in pollinating night-blooming, pale, broadly tubular or conical flowers cupping nectars rich in glucose and fructose.

Hawkmoths also prefer pale flowers that stand out at dusk, but favor strongly scented flowers with sucrose-dominated nectars concealed in deep narrow tubes. Butterflies also suck nectar from deep narrow corollas but

THE SAME LOCATION, EXACTLY ONE YEAR EARLIER, SHOWS BRITTLEBUSHES FLOWERING ON MARCH 24, 1998.
Paul Gill

may do so during the day and commonly choose flowers that are deep pink or other intense colors.

Some bees specialize in a particular shape and size of flower but rarely favor pure red blooms. Many of the favorite bee-pollinated flowers have brightly colored "landing pads" or "honey guides" that point the way to hidden nectar in the flower. Larger bumblebees and carpenter bees can open closed flowers or force themselves beneath masses of stamens to reach pools of nectar in the bases of flowers. Entering and then escaping, they often end up covered with the pollen that they carry to and rub off on the stamens of other flowers. Moths and beetles also seek particular kinds of flowers.

Plants needing migrating pollinators may not reproduce as well if their blooms fail to attract these animals. The animals themselves may lose weight for lack of nectar and reproduce less if they reach a destination before — or after — the flowers open.

For example, Arizona's ocotillos may bloom anytime between early

AN EAGER BEE (ABOVE)
TRIES ITS LUCK WITH AN
ASTER BLOSSOM.
Larry Lindahl

A HAWKMOTH, OR
SPHINX MOTH, (ABOVE
RIGHT) SIPS FROM A
SACRED DATURA.
Bruce Griffin

March and late May, but those more to the south or at lower elevations generally flower earlier than those to the north or in higher mountains. The bloom of each population usually follows, by a few days, the peak arrival time of migrating hummingbirds in that area. If cold weather elsewhere delays the hummingbirds, yet the ocotillos still bloom on time, the plants' seed set for that year can be extremely low for lack of sufficient pollination.

Wind-pollinated flowers are not as showy as those pollinated by animals. Wind-pollinated plants often possess an abundance of small, simple flowers that give a greater target area for the floating pollen than would a few more intricate ones.

As a result of such influences, we can see drought-escaping ephemeral wildflowers no bigger than a child's fingernail and others, such as sacred datura, with 6-inch-long, trumpetlike blooms. Cacti can have many unscented, miniature cup-shaped corollas or contain a solitary, 8-inch tubular perfume factory, such as that found in the night-blooming cereus.

Pollinating birds, bats, bees, and butterflies are not the only animals attracted to native wildflowers. These plants provide food, shade, shelter, and escape cover to many creatures. Although people are attracted to these plants' showy blooms for a short spurt of time each year, the plants themselves attract many animal communities all year.

THE DELICATE HUNT
The Art of Wildflower Watching

To go stalking wildflowers, what more "gear" do you need than a good pair of eyes and a willingness to drive to and walk through Arizona's wildlands? Hunting wildflowers is a little like breathing — you don't take lessons to learn how, you just do it.

Yet, one watcher can see dozens of blossoming species that someone else might glance over and pass by. The fragrance, the dance of various pollinators, and the diversity of hues associated with one wildflower species might all be missed if you are not cued to be aware of them.

After a few forays into the field, frustrations and questions can arise. Why aren't there flowers out this Easter when there were tons of them last year at this time? Do you have to drive very far? Why do the big stands of blooms seem to be on the highway right-of-way? Can you legally pick them on either side of the fence? And how do you figure out the names of the ones that you don't already know?

For starters, you can benefit from the knowledgeable eyes of veteran wildflower watchers who collaborate in the Arizona Wildflower Network, coordinated by the Desert Botanical Garden in Phoenix. Beginning the first week of March, the garden's staff compiles reports from a cooperative network of botanists, amateur naturalists, park rangers, and wilderness managers. Using a list of a hundred or so of the most common spring plants, they report the four showiest species for each accessible locale in their territory, as well as all other plants that have broken out of bud in the previous week. These reports are posted weekly during March and April on the garden's Web site (www.dbg.org/); go to the home page and click on "Wildflower Sightings." For those without Internet access, call the garden's general plant hotline — (480) 941-1225, weekdays, 10 to 11:30 A.M. — and the staff will help you.

Like going to an art museum to become familiar with the work of a famous artist, you can learn to know various wildflowers by visiting the state's botanical gardens, outdoor museums, and arboreta; they sow and show wildflowers on their own grounds. The Desert Botanical Garden, Tucson Botanical Gardens, Tohono Chul Park in northwest Tucson, the Museum of Northern Arizona, The Arboretum at Flagstaff, Boyce Thompson Southwestern Arboretum, and the Arizona-Sonora Desert Museum feature spring and summer flowering natives along their trails.

THE SONORAN DESERT COMES ALIVE WITH DESERT GLOBEMALLOWS, MEXICAN GOLDPOPPIES, AND LUPINES.
Nick Berezenko

OWL CLOVER / David W. Lazaroff

LUPINE / George Stocking

Before venturing out on a long trip to unknown ground, it may be worthwhile to familiarize yourself with the species growing in the garden nearest your home.

Believe it or not, being even slightly familiar with a few scientific names can prove helpful. Common names get applied with confusing abandon, and sometimes the easiest way to pinpoint what you're looking at or looking for is to know its scientific name — or at least have a ready source that will tell you its scientific name. Once you discover, though, that the exotic combination of genus and species can't intimidate you (just think of them as a plant's first and last names), you might even amuse yourself by delving into the details that the Latinized names can convey. For example, a plant with the species (second) name of "odorata" probably has fragrant flowers or leaves; find a plant with the species name "purpurea," and you know you'll be seeing a purple flower.

Once you decide to go on the road, you might want to also carry a few basic books and equipment as traveling companions. Although this book will get you started on how to find and identify more than 100 Arizona wildflowers, our reference list suggests various other field guides.

When you hunker down for a nose-to-petal view of some of the tiniest wildflowers, you'll understand why some call them "bellyflowers." A low-cost magnifying glass can help you sort out these colorful miniatures, since most plants are identifiable less by their leaves and more through their floral characteristics such as petal shape and number, corolla and calyx size, and shape of the inflorescence. If keeping track of all these often minuscule characteristics overwhelms you at first, take a deep breath, relax, and just open yourself up to the beautiful microscopic world of floral patterns. Enjoying their brief beauty does not depend on being able to recite what they are.

Photography opens another door to reveling in the plant world. You might want to consider carrying a camera with macro lens or magnifying attachments, a tripod, a small piece of rug or canvas in case you want to go prone next to the bellyflowers, and a piece of black velvet for a photo background.

If you are vulnerable to pollen allergies, consider taking along antihistamines and a pollen mask for any extended stays in wildflower fields. Although many of the showiest flowers have sticky, heavier pollen suited to dispersal by bees and hummingbirds, wind-pollinated grasses and herbs often grow with them. Certain flowers and their stems and leaf juices also cause contact dermatitis, so use caution if handling them. Scorpion-weeds, euphorbias, agaves, and globemallows can potentially irritate skin.

National parks and forests, as well as some Indian reservations and state, county, and city parks, require permits for any wildflower collecting. State law prohibits removal of whole plants such as mariposa lilies, agaves,

SHARING A SHELTER OF ROCKS, RED SAGE LOOMS ABOVE SOME MOUNTAIN OXEYE IN THE CHIRICAHUA MOUNTAINS. Willard Clay

and cacti. For a list of protected species, particularly endangered ones, write or call the Arizona Department of Agriculture, Attention: Native Plants, 1688 W. Adams, Phoenix, AZ 85007; (602) 364-0935; or go online to: www.agriculture.state.az.us/PSD/nativeplants.htm/.

Although permits are granted for collection and study of certain rare plants, use caution even when merely visiting the areas where they grow. Trampling can destroy unseen seedlings, and inadvertent damage to canopy plants can reduce the protective cover which immature plants need

BARREL CACTI ALONG THE TRAIL BURST INTO BLOOM NEAR SABINO CANYON. Willard Clay

as shelter from temperature extremes and from foraging predators.

On private lands, the law allows you to collect native flowers and seeds if you have the landowner's permission, but remember that over-harvesting can diminish future generations of growth. Why pick naturally occurring wildflowers when there are so many other ways to enjoy them? A little restraint will allow the next person who comes along to appreciate them as much as you have.

3

BLOOMS OF FROST
Winter & Early Spring

No flowering season in the United States compares to that of the southwestern deserts in late winter. Arizona's Sonoran and Mohave deserts erupt into a dozen different colors even when days are still short and light frosts not uncommon.

While desert plants may still face occasional wintertime freezes, Arizona's high country of the expansive Colorado Plateau hopes for snowfall as a its guarantee for springtime blooms. The more snow from Pacific Coast storms blowing in during December and January, the more spring runoff to water meadows and woodlands from the Kaibab Plateau east to the White Mountains.

Some wildflowers that bloom in two seasons, such as sand verbena, also get an early start. In warm winters, particularly in Regions 3 and 4, lupines and goldpoppies may begin to flower in late January. Yet, in most other locales, flowering still peaks after the spring equinox.

The winter wildflowers grow largely in the warmest areas, Regions 3 and 4, which also are more prone to get early winter rains, if they receive any at all. Regions 1 and 2 harbor some of the same species, but there flowering peaks much closer to the spring equinox. Timing, from one region to the next, depends on killing frosts, daytime temperature highs, and other weather variables.

Arranged in alphabetical order by scientific name, the individual plant descriptions list a primary common name in bold, some alternate common names, the scientific name (genus and species) in italics, and the plant's family name. (See page 7 for the taxonomic standard.)

A TALL SAGUARO CACTUS AND ARCHING DESERT GLOBEMALLOWS GRACE THE DESERT AT ORGAN PIPE CACTUS NATIONAL MONUMENT.
Randy A. Prentice

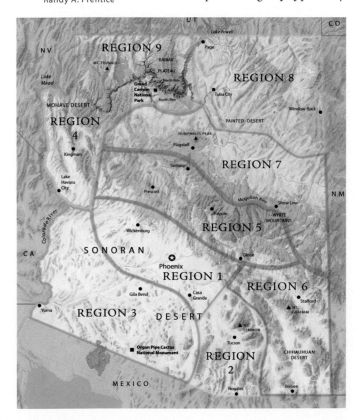

desert sand verbena

hairy sand verbena
Abronia villosa
Four O'Clock Family

Sand verbena has stalked heads of pinkish purple to rose-colored "flowers" or colored bracts. Sand often sticks to its thick leaves in the dunes and desert washes where it grows. It may bloom any time from the beginning of February to early October. There is usually one peak in flowering around mid-February, and if soil moisture persists, another peak may occur any time between May and late August.
Regions 2, 3

brownfoot

pink perezia, Wright's desertpeony
Acourtia wrightii
[*Perezia wrightii*]
Sunflower family

In bloom from January into June, this prickly desert perennial beckons with its fragrant flower clusters, but elbows back the overzealous with its stiff, spiny leaves (a petite desert cousin with similar wavy-edged leaves is commonly known as desert holly). Long stems, sometimes up to 2 feet tall, support sprays of small, two-lipped, brownish pink or lavender pink flowers. Different Indian tribes have used the leaves and roots medicinally. Brownfoot grows throughout Arizona's desert canyons and foothills and up into the highlands below 6,000 feet.
Regions 1, 2, 3, 4, 5, 6, 7, 8, 9

FAIRY DUSTER / Steve Gilb

FAIRYDUSTER / Willard Clay

DESERT MARIGOLDS / Laurence Parent

desert marigold

desert baileya, baileya del desierto
Baileya multiradiata
Sunflower Family

Blooming in spurts over a long period, this perennial herb is also the showiest common member of the sunflower group. The desert marigold's omnipresence along road sites, its long woolly stalks, and its lovely lemon-hued flowers make it unforgettable. To confirm its identity, check to see if the seeds have withered ray flowers attached to them. Its flowering flush from early March to May is best known, but it may also contribute as much as a third of the August pollen harvest by desert honeybees, indicating another late peak. Where runoff accumulates, desert marigolds bloom almost year-round throughout the desert and into some grassland habitats. In more northern regions, between elevations of 2,000 and 5,000 feet (including in the Grand Canyon), it grows as an annual.
Regions 1, 2, 3, 4, 5, 6, 7, 9

fairyduster

false mesquite, mesquitillo
Calliandra eriophylla
Pea Family

This small shrub has clustered rose-colored flowers with numerous stamens that protrude like delicate brushes beyond the length of the blossoms themselves. The stamens hold packages of pollen called polyads, each with a sticky place for attaching onto pollinators. These flowers are set in lacy, acacia-like foliage, with five to 15 pairs of leaflets. Flowering from October through April and peaking near the end of March, fairydusters can be found from rocky hillsides and canyon walls to the banks of arroyos. Butterflies, bees, and perhaps some hummingbirds pollinate it. They are often the only winter-blooming shrubs on desert mountain slopes.
Regions 1, 2, 3, 4, 5, 6

BRITTLEBUSH / Bruce Griffin

BRITTLEBUSH / Paul Gill

BRITTLEBUSH / Stewart Aitchison

brittlebush

goldenhills, white brittlebush,
incienso
Encelia farinosa
Sunflower Family

Brittlebush forms Arizona's most extensive late-winter flower show. In frost-free areas, blossoming begins in November and sometimes persists to mid-May. Flowering is most intense in March and April. Its long-stalked, sunflower-like bouquets attract many insects. Brittlebush foliage changes radically, depending upon seasonal moisture. The first new leaves after a rain will be larger and greener, but as the soil dries, the plant produces much smaller grayish leaves. These latter leaves will persist under mild drought, whereas the first ones will be dropped to reduce water loss. The stems exude a gum that can be burned as an aromatic incense, hence the Spanish name *incienso*.
Regions 1, 2, 3, 4

Mormon tea

Ephedra torreyana
Joint-Fir Family

Scientists trace this green-branched shrub to primitive plants that reproduced without flowering. Small flowerlike cones of yellowish, papery bracts cradle male stamens or female ovules, awaiting wind-carried pollen during February and March. Mormon settlers did indeed brew a tea from the stems, which often are leafless or have a few tiny, scalelike leaves. Mormon tea grows along gravelly desert slopes and dry scrublands between 4,000 and 6,000 feet.
Regions 4, 5, 7, 8, 9

filaree

storksbill, redstem stork's bill
Erodium cicutarium
Geranium Family

The delicate pink flowers and lacy, ground-hugging foliage look much at home — a noted Arizona novel even bears their name as its title — but this southern European probably came ashore with the Spanish. It blooms during February in the low deserts and the Grand Canyon's Inner Gorge, on through July in the higher elevations, and into October when above 8,500 feet. After the petals drop off, the pointed ovary lengthens into a lancelike fruit with seeds. Each seed's hard casing has a sharply pointed end and a wiry "tail" that dries into a corkscrew. When rainfall moistens the corkscrew, it uncoils in a driving spiral, working the seed into the soil.
Region 1, 2, 3, 4, 5, 6, 7, 9

MORMON TEA / Tom Danielsen

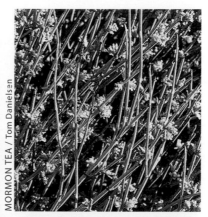

MORMON TEA / Tom Danielsen

FILAREE / Tanya Beth Kinsey

firewheel

blanketflower
Gaillardia pulchella
Sunflower Family

This gaillardia has beautiful three-lobed, petal-like ray flowers ringing the central purple-tinged disk flowers. A variable spring annual, it has basal, clustered, alternate leaves that may be both divided and toothed. The solitary flower stalks bloom as early as February at lower desert elevations and as late as July in desert grasslands and chaparral up to 4,000 feet.

Regions 1, 2, 3, 4, 5, 6

Goodding's verbena

verbena, southwestern mock vervain
Glandularia gooddingii
[*Verbena gooddingii*]
Verbena Family

Verbena's mauve or lavender flowers form large headlike clusters atop hairy perennial foliage. Enough of these plants emerge on the same bajadas, or desert slopes, and mesas to produce a carpetlike effect. Goodding's verbena can be found throughout Arizona below 5,000 feet. Forming large patches, it attracts many butterflies and moths. It blooms from February through October, but flowering peaks in late March.

Regions 1, 2, 3, 4, 5, 6

FIREWHEEL / Suzanne Holden

GOODDING'S VERBENA / Tanya Beth Kinsey

GOODDING'S VERBENA / Larry Ulrich

AJO LILY / Chuck Lawsen

ajo lily

desert lily, ajo silvestre
Hesperocallis undulata
Lily Family

The large white trumpets resemble the Easter lily. The edible bulb is reminiscent of garlic, *ajo* in Spanish. Flowers emerge from a rosette of ribbony leaves, sometimes at ground level, at other times on a stalk up to 3 feet tall. The flower's deep spurs, filled with nectar, attract pollinating sphinx moths. Most common and larger in moisture-laden dune areas, this lily also inhabits gravel flats below 2,000 feet. It blooms from mid-February to mid-April, peaking in late March.
Regions 1, 2, 3, 4

chuparosa

beloperone
Justicia californica
Acanthus Family

This sprawling, pale-stemmed shrub produces enough tubular red flowers to tide over most hummingbirds through the winter until other plants begin to bloom. Frequenting the sand and gravel washes skirting low desert mountains, chuparosa always grows below 2,500 feet. Starting in late summer, its bloom time extends through the winter, from late August through June, depending upon the locale.
Regions 1, 2, 3

CHUPAROSA / Suzanne Holden

CHUPAROSA / Robert G. McDonald

CREOSOTE BUSH / Suzanne Holden

BLADDERPOD MUSTARD / Dave Bly

BLADDERPOD MUSTARD / Paul Gill

creosote bush

creosotebush, greasewood
Larrea tridentata
Caltrop Family

These strong-scented, resinous shrubs form extensive stands throughout the warm deserts of the Americas. Although the yellow, five-petalled flowers are small, they offer color where drought eliminates other hues. The 5,000 to 50,000 flowers produced by a single creosote bush in an average year attract bees, wasps, and flies. Petals twist 90 degrees once they have been pollinated. Sonoran Desert creosote blooms peak in March and April and again in November through December. Creosote grows on flats, bajadas, and hills below 4,500 feet.
Regions 1, 2, 3, 4, 6

bladderpod mustard

Gordon's bladderpod
Lesquerella gordonii
Mustard Family

A golden-flowered miniature, this early annual forms enormous stands by itself during years when rainfall is so low that other flowers fail. It prefers plains and open valleys of the deserts and adjacent grasslands. Bladderpod extends into other habitats as well. Several species of these mustards have been evaluated as desert crops because of their unusual vegetable oil quality and potential industrial uses. They bloom and are bee-pollinated from mid-February to mid-April.
Regions 2, 3, 4, 5, 6, 9

Mojave lupine

desert lupine, Coulter's lupine
Lupinus sparsiflorus
Pea Family

This annual lupine species has violet blue, pealike blooms with yellow spots on one petal that turns purplish red after bees have manipulated the flower. The fingerlike leaflets tilt to track the sun at a direct angle, thereby gaining additional solar radiation during the winter when such energy is at a premium. Some years, lupine begins to flower in January. Attractive to bumblebees and digger bees, these flowers peak in color and fragrance, from mid-March through mid-April, on alluvial fans, washes, and canyons below 2,300 feet.
Regions 1, 2, 3, 4, 5, 6

blazingstar

whitebract blazingstar, white bract stickleaf
Mentzelia involucrata
Stick Leaf Family

A short-stemmed flower, colored cream or lemon, this is one of numerous western wildflowers given the name "blazingstar." Each flower emerges from a set of narrow-lobed bracts (specialized leaves) coming off the whitish stems. Although other stickleafs will flower along sandy washes in early summer or fall, this species adds its color to the desert between February and April and is spent by summer.
Regions 1, 3, 9

BLAZINGSTAR / Suzanne Holden

MOJAVE LUPINE / Michael Collier

MOJAVE LUPINE / Jerry Sieve

purple mat

leafy nama, purplemat
Nama demissum
Waterleaf Family

As its name implies, this low-growing annual forms mats of branching, hairy, prostrate stems. The tubular flowers, in bloom from February to May, add a delightful touch of purplish pink against the clays and sandy soils of Arizona's deserts.

Regions 1, 2, 3, 4, 8

desert evening primrose

desert evening-primrose, bottle evening primrose
Oenothera primiveris
Evening Primrose Family

This low-growing desert annual, anchored by its taproot, is a true evening bloomer. Each flower's four notched, yellow petals open wide in the evening, so that nocturnal hawkmoths seeking nectar can pollinate them, and then close the next morning, fading to a purplish hue as the flower ages. The short flower stems barely rise above flattened rosettes of long greenish gray leaves that are divided into broad, rounded lobes, sometimes with reddish stems. Desert evening primrose blooms in Arizona from mid-February to May at low elevations along desert washes and on sandy plains and in the Grand Canyon.

Regions 1, 2, 3, 4, 6, 8, 9

PURPLE MAT / Jeff Snyder

DESERT EVENING PRIMROSE / Randy A. Prentice

SCORPION-WEED / Ralph Lee Hopkins

SCORPION-WEED / Chuck Lawsen

scorpion-weed

caterpillarweed
Phacelia crenulata
Waterleaf Family

Violet purple, on rare occasions white, these flowers form on one side of a curled branch in a manner suggestive of a scorpion's tail. Scorpion-weeds are sticky annual plants with ill-scented, highly divided, oblong leaves. The duration of their flowering season may range from a week in a dry year to eight weeks in a wet one. Peak bloom time varies from late March to late April, when it is extremely common from grassland mesas down into low deserts. It also grows in the Grand Canyon.

Regions 1, 3, 4, 5, 9

CANAIGRE / Tanya Beth Kinsey

CANAIGRE / Tanya Beth Kinsey

CANAIGRE / Stewart Aitchison

canaigre

canaigre dock, desert rhubarb
Rumex hymenosepalus
Buckwheat Family

Bright green stands of canaigre in roadside fields often catch the eye, but more for the lush leaves (up to 2 feet long and 4 inches wide) than for the greenish white flowers. A moisture-loving perennial throughout Arizona at elevations from 1,000 to 6,000 feet, canaigre (said *can-IH-gray*) doesn't grow roots, but it sinks long tubers deep into moist, sandy soils along streambeds, pools, and well-watered meadows. The tubers give rise to broad, lance-shaped leaves and thick, fleshy stems, 1 to 3 feet high, that support dense flower clusters. Flowering starts as early as February, extending into March and April in southern Arizona and into June going north as far as Lake Powell's canyons.
Regions 1, 2, 3, 5, 7, 8, 9

jojoba

goatnut, coffee berry, deernut
Simmondsia chinensis
Jojoba Family

Although this desert shrub lacks showy flowers, its floral clusters and waxy fruit still intrigue many people. The plant shape guides wind-dispersed pollen toward female flowers, but bees also steal pollen from male plants. Jojoba prefers rocky slopes with coarse soils, above pockets of cold air drainage. The liquid wax extracted from its seeds has been a key ingredient in cosmetics. Jojoba has a long and variable flowering season. At one site, it has extended from mid-January to late April in some years, but only from February to early March in others.
Regions 1, 2, 3, 6

JOJOBA / Suzanne Holden

JOJOBA / Suzanne Holden

DESERT GLOBEMALLOW / Gary Ladd

DESERT GLOBEMALLOW / Tom Danielsen

desert globemallow

desert mallow, sore-eye
poppy, mal de ojo
Sphaeralcea ambigua
Mallow Family

The large number of orange flowers that this multi-stemmed mallow produces over a year steadily provides pollen and nectar to honeybees and mallow-specializing bees. Flower color variants include white, purple, red, and grenadine hues. A low-growing perennial herb, desert globemallow has long panicles of flowers and roundish, shallow-lobed leaves. The leaves' star-shaped hairs irritate the eyes if accidentally rubbed into them. Growing from dry rocky slopes to washes and the banks of springs, this is one of the most adaptable mallows, which seldom exhibit so much drought tolerance. Below 3,500 feet, this species blooms year-round.

Regions 1, 2, 3, 4, 5, 6, 9

WILD AWAKENING
Mid-spring

Mid-spring offers the greatest diversity of ephemeral, or short-lived, annual wildflowers of any season in Arizona. For the deserts, it is also Arizona's best known flowering season, since many visitors on spring breaks take desert drives or hikes between late March and mid-April when these flowers usually are peaking. In the high country, what snow remains lies at the highest elevations, but even where no snow has lingered, some danger from frost remains. In the northern regions, certain warmer, sheltered microclimates — along lower elevations and down in canyons — now show spring colors earlier than in the rest of the zone.

This season begins by the spring equinox in Regions 1 to 4, since the last killing frost has passed by then. The nights remain cool, but the sunny days warm up enough to bring out solitary bees to begin pollination. March and April wildflowers generally need the longer days to trigger flowering. There are some late-winter flowers still blooming, as well as widespread shows of annual flowers that bloom now in the deserts and will show up later as summer wildflowers in the cooler, non-desert areas.

Region 5 remains cold enough that only small flowers such as namas, drabas, and lotuses can be seen. Forest and woodland plant communities across Regions 7, 8, and 9 can see their last frost (depending on elevation) anytime from early to late May and sometimes into June.

Arranged in alphabetical order by scientific name, the individual plant descriptions list a primary common name in bold, some alternate common names, the scientific name (genus and species) in italics, and the plant's family name. (See page 7 for the taxonomic standard.)

CRIMSON
MONKEYFLOWERS SHOW
THEIR LIVELY FACES IN
OAK CREEK CANYON.
Ralph Lee Hopkins

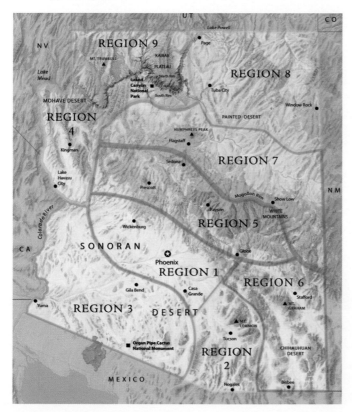

largeflower onion

desert wild onion, Arizona onion
Allium macropetalum
Lily Family

A wild food source smelling and tasting like cultivated onions, the small, strongly flavored bulbs and their long, grasslike leaves give rise to waxy, starlike flowers clustered at the stem tips. Each flower's six pointed petals, colored a soft white or pale pink, have a single deep crease lined with a pink or reddish stripe. You can find the plants blossoming from March to June on desert flats and rocky foothills from 1,000- to 7,000-foot elevations.
Regions 1, 2, 3, 5, 6, 8

golden columbine

yellow columbine
Aquilegia chrysantha
Buttercup Family

This five-petaled flower, with its long, distinctive spurs, can flare to 3 inches wide. It is Arizona's most abundant and widely growing columbine, found mainly in the pine-forest belt at elevations up to 11,000 feet, but also growing to as low as 3,000 feet if along streams or in moist crevices of the Grand Canyon. It blooms from April through September.
Regions 4, 2, 6, 7, 9

LARGEFLOWER ONIONS / Gary Ladd

GOLDEN COLUMBINE / Marty Cordano

GOLDEN COLUMBINE / George Stocking

PRICKLY POPPY / Willard Clay

PRICKLY POPPY / Tom Danielsen

prickly poppy

southwestern pricklepoppy,
cowboys' fried egg
Argemone pleiacantha
Poppy Family

A plant that truly earns its name, this poppy has nasty spines on it stems, leaves, and sepals. The white, crinkled-tissue skirt of four to six showy petals surrounds many golden or bright orange stamens, looking for all the world like a fried egg. Blooming from April to November, the eyecatching flowers sometimes grow as high as 3 feet along roads and in fields, mesas, and washes from 1,400 to 8,000 feet.
Regions 1, 2, 3, 5, 6, 7, 9

desert mariposa lily

red mariposa, sego lily
Calochortus kennedyi
Lily Family

This striking spring bloomer can be differentiated from other mariposas by its deep orange-red to yellow or vermilion velvety petals, each with a brownish purple spot at the base. In some places, mariposas are beetle-pollinated. The desert mariposa has clusters of two to four flowers on a stalk rising from a bulb hidden beneath linear, basal leaves. In Arizona, its blossoming is largely limited to April, peaking in mid-month. It is found in many habitats, from desert to grassland and semi-arid woodland vegetation. A related mariposa species, *Calochortus nuttallii*, commonly flowers from May to July on the Grand Canyon's North and South rims.
Regions 1, 2, 3, 4, 5, 6 *Calochortus kennedyi*
Region 9 *Calochortus nuttallii*

DESERT MARIPOSA LILY / David W. Lazaroff

DESERT MARIPOSA LILY / Larry Ulrich

owl clover

exserted Indian paintbrush, escobita
Castilleja exserta
[*Orthocarpus purpurascens*]
Figwort Family

In southern Arizona, owl clover cloaks large areas with purple for a few weeks each wet spring. This color is as much a function of the bracts beneath each flower as it is of the sepals and petals themselves. Its flowering spikes vary from hot purplish pink to velvety red violet with yellow spots. Alone or in mixed stands, this annual inhabits plains, mesas, and slopes of deserts and grasslands between 1,500 and 4,500 feet. Early April is the best time to catch its color, but flowering may be just beginning then or may already be in its fourth week.
Regions 1, 2, 3, 4, 5, 6

California redbud

western redbud, Texas redbud
Cercis canadensis var. *texensis*
[*Cercis occidentalis*]
Pea Family

This attractive deciduous shrub, common to the Grand Canyon's Inner Gorge and to the sandstone canyonlands of northern Arizona, may grow as a small tree up to 12 feet tall. Sheltered in their canyon habitats near water sources like streams and seeps, redbuds burst into bloom with showy, bright rose flowers as early as March. Glossy, lobed, 4-inch-wide leaves will emerge later, and the redbuds will continue blooming and leafing out on into May.
Regions 7, 9

OWL CLOVER / Larry Lindahl

OWL CLOVER / Chuck Lawsen

CALIFORNIA REDBUD / Gary Ladd

CALIFORNIA REDBUD / George H. H. Huey

desert willow

desertwillow, desert catalpa, mimbre
Chilopsis linearis
Bignonia Family

Although this tree has narrow, lancelike leaves like a willow, its flowers smell more like violets and look more like orchids. White, lavender, and yellow background colors flaunt sprinklings of dots, blotches, and streaks representing the whole color spectrum. These large blooms draw bees and hummingbirds Although they frequent desert washes, desert willows become abundant at higher elevations (up to about 5,000 feet) in grasslands and oak-juniper woodlands. Blooming usually begins in April, and the tree continues flowering, sometimes until early October.
Regions 1, 4, 5, 6, 7, 9

feather dalea

feathery dalea, featherplume, indigo bush
Dalea formosa
Pea Family

Bees pollinate the deep reddish purple, pealike flowers clustering above this plant's dark green, pinnate leaflets. The dalea blooms March to June along rocky foothills, mountains, and dry plains between 2,000 and 6,500 feet.
Regions 2, 5, 6, 7

barestem larkspur

tall mountain larkspur, espuelita
Delphinium scaposum
Buttercup Family

This gorgeous larkspur emerges on a leafless stalk rising from a basal cluster of angled leaf blades and a woody root stalk. Its sepals are an intense royal blue, its two-toothed spur bronze or purple, and its true petals blue or white with bluish tips. Larkspurs occur in sizable colonies, where bumblebees and hummingbirds may fight each other for control of nectar-rich territories. They flower March to May on mesas, knolls, and hillsides, from low deserts up to 7,000 feet in the pine zone.
Regions 1, 2, 3, 4, 5, 6, 9

Engelmann's hedgehog cactus

strawberry hedgehog, strawberry cactus
Echinocereus engelmannii
Cactus Family

The hedgehog's reddish purple or magenta flowers rupture the skin of this cactus just above the areoles, the places where two to six central spines cluster along the plant's ribs. The curved spines vary in color, from white or gold to black. Its cup-shaped flowers open for several consecutive days, attracting bees and beetles to their abundant pollen and nectar. Medium-sized bees alight on the stigma and probe into the masses of pollen below. As a bee collects one flower's pollen, it leaves behind other pollen, aiding cross-pollination. Hedgehog cactus blooms often last only two weeks, beginning at the end of March or as late as mid-April. It grows on outwash fans, flats, and hillsides from sea level to 5,000 feet in grasslands and in the Grand Canyon.
Regions 1, 2, 3, 4, 5, 9

LARKSPUR / David W. Lazaroff

LARKSPUR / David W. Lazaroff

HEDGEHOG CACTUS / Chuck Lawsen

HEDGEHOG CACTUS / Jack Dykinga

MEXICAN GOLD POPPY / David W. Lazaroff

APACHE PLUME / Suzanne Holden

MEXICAN GOLD POPPY / Tom Danielsen

APACHE PLUME / Suzanne Holden

Mexican goldpoppy

Mexican goldenpoppy, goldpoppy
Eschscholtzia californica ssp. *mexicana*
[*Eschscholtzia mexicana*]
Poppy Family

Easily the Sonoran Desert's most-photographed annual wildflower, this poppy's petals are usually gold to orange, almost indistinguishable from its close cousin, the California poppy. In fact, the goldpoppy is now considered a subspecies of the California poppy, although some botanists once classed it as its own species. Sometimes white and pink mutants bloom amidst large golden stands. The highly dissected, lacy foliage gives rise to solitary-stalked, four-petalled blooms on plains, bajadas, and mountain slopes below 4,500 feet. Blooming begins in mid-February in warmer locales like Phoenix and Yuma, but is more limited to March and April near Tucson and Tumacacori.
Regions 1, 2, 3, 4, 5, 6

Apache plume

Apacheplume, feather rose
Fallugia paradoxa
Rose Family

The Apache plume's broad, white flowers, with their multiple yellow stamens, look much like wild roses. They bloom from April to October before fruiting into seeds with long, whitish or pink plumes. Look for this evergreen shrub from 3,500 to 8,000 feet in chaparral regions of the upper desert, along roadsides and dry washes, and at the Grand Canyon (on both rims and in the Inner Gorge).
Regions 1, 2, 3, 4, 5, 6, 7, 8, 9

ocotillo

candlewood, coachwhip
Fouquieria splendens
Ocotillo Family

The five waxy petals of each flower form a nectar-laden tube on the ocotillo's wandlike, thorny stems. Ocotillos range widely across rocky slopes in grasslands and deserts below 4,500 feet. Usually synchronous with the spring migration of hummingbirds, ocotillo populations bloom progressively from south to north and from low to high elevations. Each stand offers nectar for three to six weeks. Statewide, the blooming extends from early March through late May. The flowers' scarlet tubes attract carpenter bees and specific hummingbird species: Anna's, black-chinned, broad-billed, broad-tailed, Costa's, and rufous. After a good rain, the leaves emerge and the green stems expand. With drought, the leaves drop off to reduce water loss. Southwesterners occasionally plant ocotillos as living fences.
Regions 1, 2, 3, 4, 5, 6

desert sunflower

desertgold, hairy
desertsunflower
Geraea canescens
Sunflower Family

The fuzzy-leaved, desert sunflower reaches heights of 2 feet in gravelly washes and sandy flats in lower desert areas. Its large, yellow radiate heads are showy and aromatic, attracting both bees and hawkmoths (sometimes called "hummingbird moths"). Bees that gather its nectar daily also use evening primrose pollen. Desert sunflowers tolerate some disturbance and active sand movement in dune fields found below 3,000 feet in elevation. Flowering is most obvious in early April but may extend from January to July in certain locales.
Regions 1, 2, 3, 4

OCOTILLO / Robert G. McDonald

DESERT SUNFLOWER / Suzanne Holden

GOLDFIELDS / Suzanne Holden

goldfields

California goldfields, baeria
Lasthenia californica
[*Lasthenia chrysostoma*]
Sunflower Family

This low-growing, tiny-flowered annual has linear, opposite leaves and forms small clumps or large carpets after good winter rains. Its small, yellow, terminal heads seldom reach 6 inches in height. Found on mesas and plains from 1,500 to 4,500 feet in elevation, goldfields can carpet sandy flats for weeks. They bloom as early as February and as late as mid-April but peak in the middle of March.
Regions 1, 2, 3, 5, 6

blue flax

Lewis flax, prairie flax
Linum lewisii
Flax Family

The delicate blue flowers, their five broad petals finely ribbed with a darker shade, balance on slender stems above threadlike leaves before wilting and dropping off by midday. Blooming March to September, the flowers sometimes come out white. This long-blooming perennial is common on open mesas and in conifer forests from 3,500 to 9,500 feet and goes into flower from March to September.
Regions 2, 4, 5, 6, 7, 9

BLUE FLAX / Tom Bean

BLUE FLAX / Stewart Aitchison

climbing snapdragon

roving sailor, violet snapdragon vine
Maurandella antirrhiniflora
[*Maurandya antirrhiniflora*]
Figwort Family

This perennial vine twines, ivylike, around and over boulders and bushes, sometimes up through branches as high as 8 feet, and blooms from April into October. Look for its leathery, three-pointed, arrow-shaped leaves in piñon-juniper woodlands, on sandy plains, and along rocky slopes and washes between 1,500 and 6,000 feet. Like oversized snapdragon flowers hung singly from threadlike stems, the vivid blooms range from pale lavender and darker violet to reddish pink, even scarlet, with white or yellowish throats. Pollinating bumblebees push through the flaring lobes into the tubular corolla to reach the nectar at the bottom.
Regions 2, 3, 4, 5, 6, 7

plains blackfoot daisy

plains blackfoot, blackfoot daisy
Melampodium leucanthum
Sunflower Family

A dependably blooming daisy with white, purple-veined ray flowers, this species is a perennial herb or subshrub. Its many flower heads range from a little more than an inch in radius to about a third that size. Whatever it lacks in flower size it makes up in persistence, with some flowering from mid-March through to December. On drier limestone slopes in southern Arizona, however, flowering peaks in late March and doesn't last past September. These daisies can be found in desert grassland and oak woodland between elevations of 2,000 and 5,000 feet.
Regions 1, 2, 4, 5, 6

CLIMBING SNAPDRAGON / Larry Ulrich

PLAINS BLACKFOOT DAISY / Suzanne Holden

yellow monkeyflower

common monkeyflower, seep
monkeyflower
Mimulus guttatus
Figwort Family

A moisture-loving perennial that can stretch to 3 feet tall, this monkeyflower can be found blooming, March to September, along streams and around canyon seeps and springs between 500 and 9,500 feet. The bright yellow flowers have two lips, with two flaring lobes above and three below, leading to a hairy throat blotched and stippled with reddish pink to scarlet. Its relative, the crimson or scarlet monkeyflower (*Mimulus cardinalis*), grows in many of the same shady streamside habitats but not at elevations below 2,000 feet; it blooms from March to October.

Regions 2, 3, 4, 6, 7, 9 *Mimulus guttatus*
Regions 2, 4, 6, 7, 9 *Mimulus cardinalis*

manyflowered four o'clock

Colorado four o'clock
Mirabilis multiflora
Four O'Clock Family

Named for its tendency to open its magenta purple, funnel-shaped flowers in the late afternoon, only to wither by the next morning, this perennial grows its rubbery, sticky leaves in a densely clumped mound. You can find it blooming, April to September, on hillsides and mesas throughout much of Arizona from elevations of 2,500 to 6,500 feet. Regions 1, 2, 3, 4, 5, 6, 7, 8, 9

purple prickly pear

purple pricklypear, longspine pricklypear
Opuntia macrocentra
[*Opuntia violacea*]
Cactus Family

With purple-tinged pads and opaque, red brown spines, this prickly pear cactus is easy to distinguish from other prickly pear species. The plant's brilliant yellow flowers glow against the red violet hues of its pads and spines. One variety's golden flowers have red centers. As far as we know, this is the only Arizona prickly pear from which Indian tribes ate the floral buds, rather than the fruit. Purple prickly pears are found from 2,000 to 5,000 feet in the Sonoran and Chihuahuan deserts and the grassland-woodland bridge between them. Flowers begin to open in early April, continuing through late May. Bees must crawl beneath pollen-laden stamens to reach the nectar.
Regions 2, 5, 6

MANYFLOWERED FOUR O'CLOCK / Larry Lindahl

PURPLE PRICKLY PEAR / Randy A. Prentice

dwarf lousewort

juniper lousewort, wood betony
Pedicularis centranthera
Figwort Family

These oddly colored, low-growing perennials are partially root-parasitic. The stoutly tubular flowers are mostly whitish or palest pink, shading up to two purplish lobed lips. The surrounding long, grayish green leaves grow in a basal rosette, their finely cut lobes along the reddish midrib looking like a heavily ruffled fern against the fallen pine needles of forest floors between 5,000 and 8,000 feet. Dwarf lousewort blooms from April to June.
Regions 1, 2, 4, 5, 7, 8, 9

Parry's penstemon

Parry's beardtongue
Penstemon parryi
Figwort Family

A spray of these rose magenta, funnel-shaped flowers can make any landscape especially memorable. They are even more attractive to bees and to Anna's and Costa's hummingbirds, which use them as one of their four or five major nectar sources in the spring. Flowering time is rather reliable, beginning the first week in March, peaking in late March, and lasting seven or eight weeks nearly every year. The flowers are on long stalks underlain by pale green, arrow-shaped leaves. This species favors rocky bajada slopes, desert grasslands, and mountain canyons from 1,500 to 5,000 feet, but often is dispersed widely in its landscape, rather than clumped.
Regions 1, 2, 5, 6

Santa Catalina phlox

Santa Catalina Mountain
phlox, desert phlox
Phlox tenuifolia
Phlox Family

These perennial, slightly woody herbs form tufts or mats in open desert areas, with the flowers shooting up to 2 to 3 feet high. The white and lavender funnel-shaped flowers of the desert phlox are unique for this genus of plants and are probably pollinated by moths. They add sweet and musky scents to rocky slopes between 1,500 and 5,000 feet and are known only in Arizona. They bloom from mid-March to early May, peaking before April.
Regions 1, 2, 5, 6

Woodhouse's phlox

woody phlox
Phlox speciosa ssp. *woodhousei*
Phlox Family

Woodhouse's phlox blooms in spring and again in the fall, its clusters of deep pink flowers pushing through the pine needles and leaf litter carpeting open woodlands and pine forests between elevations of 3,500 and 8,000 feet. The tubular flowers end at right-angled, deeply notched petal lobes set around a white central "eye." While the petals are sometimes all white, usually they're pink on top and white below. Shiny and thick, the dark green, oblong leaves extend stiffly from the plant's woody base, reaching up to 6 inches high.
Region 5, 7

SANTA CATALINA PHLOX / Bernadette Heath

WOODHOUSE'S PHLOX / Jack Dykinga

CLIFF ROSE / Larry Lindahl

CLIFF ROSE / Stewart Aitchison

cliffrose

Stansbury cliffrose, quinine bush, buckbrush
Purshia stansburiana
[*Cowania mexicana* var. *stansburiana*]
Rose Family

Arching gnarled branches over the rocky slopes where it lives, this evergreen's single trunk may grow into a wide, 8-foot-tall shrub or into a small tree 25 feet high. It ranges from elevations as low as 3,500 feet, in the Mohave Desert and Sonoran Desert uplands, up to 8,000 feet across the oak-piñon-juniper and pine woodlands of Regions 7 and 9 (in the Grand Canyon's Inner Gorge and on both rims). Thickly clustering along the branches after a substantial rain, the fragrant flowers open five cream or light yellow petals to about a half-inch to 1 inch wide. Flowering generally starts in April on the warmer desert uplands — in June on the higher North Rim — and continues sometimes through September. Cliffrose fruits add a new dimension: Each tiny fruit, or achene, flaunts a white, feathery tail.

Regions 1, 2, 4, 5, 7, 9

desert chicory

desert chickory, New Mexico plumeseed, desert dandelion
Rafinesquia neomexicana
Sunflower Family

A white-flowered spring bloomer, this annual shares a few superficial features with the blue-flowered perennial chicory introduced from Europe and now widespread throughout much of America. Desert chicory is short but profusely branching and has deeply divided, arrow-shaped leaves. In wet winters, it becomes abundant upon plains, gentle bajadas, and mesas, from 200 feet in the desert to its grassland edge above 3,000 feet. In some dry years, it may fail to bloom altogether even when other herbs flower. Its bloom time may stretch from March to May. Regions 1, 2, 3, 4, 5, 6, 9

skunkbush sumac

skunkbush, lemonade sumac
Rhus trilobata
Cashew or Sumac Family

A woody shrub mainly of the piñon-juniper areas and canyons, mesas, and slopes between 2,500 and 7,500 feet, this sumac is known for a citrus-tasting drink that the Apaches made from its berries. In fact, the Hopi, Hualapai, Havasupai, and Yavapai tribes all made use of its sticky, bright red berries. Before the sumac fruits, though, the mounding bush blooms with small yellow flowers from March to June. The inconspicuous, spikelike clusters of flowers appear before the foliage does, which may be fortunate — the harmless sumac's dark, shiny, three-lobed leaves bear a nasty resemblance to its intimidating cousin, poison ivy. Regions 5, 7, 8, 9

chia

desert chia, desert sage
Salvia columbariae
Mint Family

Ranging from sky blue to indigo and popular with many bees, chia flowers cluster like rings on terminal spikes above a highly divided foliage. Plant height varies from 6 inches to 18 inches, depending upon available moisture. This annual's seeds contain mucilage that gels up when they are placed in water, forming a sticky, inflated mass. This allows the seeds to stick to a site once rainfall has begun providing enough moisture to germinate. Chias bloom from sea level to 4,500 feet at the desert edge, from early March to July.

Regions 1, 2, 3, 4, 6

CHIA / Paul Gil

CHIA / Jack Dykinga

MEXICAN ELDERBERRY / Suzanne Holden

Mexican elderberry

elderberry, tapiro, blue elder
Sambucus nigra ssp. *canadensis*
[*Sambucus mexicana*]
Honeysuckle Family

As a large tree with opposite, divided leaves and flat-topped clusters of white blossoms, this Arizona wildflower is quite distinct from all others so far mentioned. This is the only elder in the state that reaches beyond the mountains. It has many different pollinators, making it a generalist. Both the flowers and fruits have been used as folk medicines, and when cooked, the fruits are edible or suitable for wine-making. The Mexican elderberry flowers from March into early July. It frequently grows next to streams and irrigation ditches.
Regions 1, 2, 3, 4, 5, 6

desert senna

Coves' cassia
Senna covesii
[*Cassia covesii*]
Pea Family

The desert senna is an herb with rusty yellow flowers rising from woody perennial stalks. It inhabits dry, rocky slopes and mesas, adding golden hues to early summer and late fall when few other shrubs bloom. Nearly every year, it can be found flowering somewhere between mid-April and mid-November; sometimes a few flowers open in March or even earlier. The nectarless flowers are "buzz-pollinated" by bees, which use their flight muscles to vibrate the pollen free from the anthers.
Regions 1, 2, 3, 4, 5, 6, 9

DESERT SENNA / Suzanne Holden

golden crownbeard

butter daisy, hierba de la bruja
Verbesina encelioides
Sunflower Family

This long-season annual has triangular, toothed grayish green leaves that are smelly. Crownbeard's broad, triple-notched ray flowers, colored a gorgeous yellow orange, surround a center of yellow disk flowers. The disk flowers ripen into flattened seeds covered with fine, grayish brown hairs (hence the name crownbeard). This plant colonizes disturbed roadsides and abandoned fields, from deserts into the pine forests, at elevations from 3,000 to about 7,000 feet. One set of these plants germinates early, to flower between March and July. A larger crop germinates with the late summer rains and flowers from July through December.
Regions 1, 2, 3, 4, 5, 6, 7, 8, 9

Joshua tree

izote de desierto, yucca
Yucca brevifolia
Agave Family

The tall, shaggy-barked Joshua tree produces gangly clusters of leaves that are relatively wide-ridged and have a coarse-toothed edge. Short flower stalks arise from the ends of its leafy branches. Forests of these plants are best known north and west of Wickenburg, on rocky plains and hillsides. The plant's short bloom time is seldom more than three weeks, but the simultaneous bloom of so many large, pale green flowers lights up the desert in March and April. The yucca moth gathers pollen, crams it on the stigma, and then lays its eggs in the developing fruit.
Regions 1, 3, 4

JOSHUA TREE / Peter Ensenberger

GOLDEN CROWNBEARD / Suzanne Holden

JOSHUA TREE / Bruce Griffin

5

COLOR FRENZY
Late Spring & Early Summer

Beginning in late April, daytime desert temperatures can exceed 95 degrees, sometimes reaching 100 degrees. Evaporation increases rapidly, and the superficial soil moisture disappears. Shallow-rooted ephemerals wither and die, leaving woody perennials and succulents to make up what little desert ground cover there is. Because the desert often receives no rain from late April through early July, it surprises some people that anything would bloom during this season of greatest water deficits.

Yet many deep-rooted trees and succulent plants in the Sonoran Desert do time their flowering so that ripened seeds will be ready to germinate as soon as the first summer rains come.

ROCKY MOUNTAIN
IRISES STAND AGAINST
A FIELD OF FALSE
HELLEBORE IN THE
MOUNT BALDY
WILDERNESS. Paul Gill

The lower elevations in Regions 5, 7, 8, and 9 also have started to warm up, even though the potential exists for a last frost as late as May or early June. Above 4,500 feet, where soil moisture lingers, spring wildflowers persist into early June.

Arranged in alphabetical order by scientific name, the individual plant descriptions list a primary common name in bold, some alternate common names, the scientific name (genus and species) in italics, and the plant's family name. (See page 7 for the taxonomic standard.)

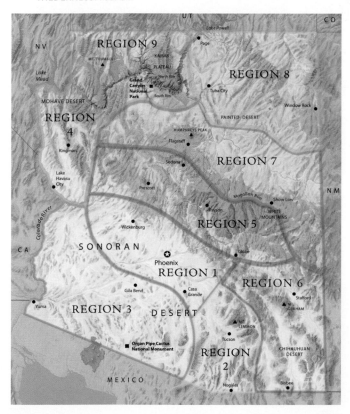

woolly locoweed

purple locoweed, woolly milkvetch
Astragalus mollissimus
Pea Family

The beauty and fragrance of the locoweed's stemless, reddish purple pealike flowers belie its toxicity to livestock. Silvery green pinnate leaves — woolly leaflets set in pairs down the lengths of long, arching midribs — clump around the flower racemes, which bloom in early summer. Found in desert scrub, piñon-juniper, and pine forests at elevations from 3,300 to 7,000 feet, this perennial can grow to a foot high and spread to 2 feet wide.
Regions 5, 7, 8, 9

saguaro

giant cactus, sahuaro
Carnegiea gigantea
Cactus Family

This unmistakable columnar cactus stands as the iconic plant of the eastern Sonoran Desert. Bee researchers have shown that a saguaro produces an average of 300 trumpetlike flowers a season. Bats, once the saguaro's prime pollinators, have decreased due to pesticides and habitat loss, but bees have taken over pollination and now account for most of the cactus's fruit set. Saguaros grow mostly on rocky hillsides and in coarse gravels of sloping desert foothills. Three-fourths of the flowering occurs within six weeks, usually between late May and early July. However, a few blooms may start in early April, and infrequent stragglers open into the fall.
Regions 1, 2, 3, 4, 5, 6

WOOLLY LOCOWEED / Bernadette Heath

SAGUARO BLOSSOM / Chuck Lawsen

SAGUARO / David H. Smith

SACRED DATURA / Michael Collier

SACRED DATURA / Stewart Aitchison

SACRED DATURA / Larry Lindahl

CLARETCUP HEDGEHOG / Jack Dykinga

CLARETCUP HEDGEHOG / Michael Collier

CLARETCUP HEDGEHOG / Jack Dykinga

sacred datura

jimsonweed, sacred
thornapple
Datura wrightii
[*Datura meteloides*]
Nightshade Family

A perennial datura, this widespread poisonous flower has fragrant, white trumpet flowers flushed a purple or lavender in the throat. Its spiny, apple-shaped capsules open irregularly to drop their buff-colored seeds. Daturas, pollinated by both hawkmoths and honeybees, have a long but irregular blooming season. This deep-rooted drought tolerator inhabits sandy flats and arroyos. A new flush of flowers opens after any substantial rain between April and November.
Regions 1, 2, 4, 5, 6, 7, 8, 9

claretcup hedgehog

Mojave mound cactus, claret
cup cactus
Echinocereus triglochidiatus
Cactus Family

At higher elevations of Arizona's deserts, between 4,000 and 9,000 feet, look for this ground-hugging cactus along gravelly slopes, on rocky hillsides, and up on cliff ledges. The densely spined, cylindrical stems (no more than 10 inches tall) look too forbidding to ever welcome delicate pollinators, especially since they may grow in mounding colonies of dozens, even hundreds, of stems. However, the funnel-shaped flowers perfectly suit a hummingbird's bill or hawkmoth's proboscis, and the blooms' various hues — red to scarlet to orange red — are most alluring to a hummingbird. From May to July, the large, cupped flowers bloom near the stem tips, displaying red stamens and green stigmas.
Regions 1, 2, 3, 4, 6, 8, 9

CHAPARRAL FLEABANE / Larry Lindahl

HAIRY GOLDEN ASTER / Larry Ulrich

chaparral fleabane

fleabane
Erigeron oreophilus
Sunflower Family

True to its name, this daisylike perennial grows in oak chaparral and open pine forests, between 3,600 and 9,500 feet. The leggy, hairy stems may grow to 16 inches, with narrowly lobed, hairy, grayish green leaves alternating up their length. Small flower heads, blooming from May to October, display a center of yellow disk flowers surrounded by many white, very narrow ray flowers.

Regions 1, 2, 5, 6, 7, 8, 9

hairy goldenaster

hairy false goldenaster, hairy false goldaster
Heterotheca villosa
Sunflower Family

The hairy goldenaster's tolerance for drought shows in its small, woolly leaves of gray to grayish green. Mounding close to the ground or growing up to 30 inches tall, this Colorado Plateau perennial sprawls on dry slopes and plains from 1,500 to 8,500 feet, including the North Rim. Loved by butterflies, it blooms May to October with abundant clusters of small, daisylike flower heads — many bright yellow, oblong ray flowers encircling dark yellow or orange yellow disk flowers.

Regions 2, 5, 7, 8, 9

skyrocket gilia

scarlet gilia, skunk flower,
polecat plant
Ipomopsis aggregata
[*Gilia aggregata*]
Phlox Family

If blooming early enough at the lower elevations, the fireburst twinkles of red on the forest floor may signal to migrating hummingbirds. The showy flowers mean nectar, even when the hues vary from the standard brilliant red to pale salmon or deep pink, with cream mottling at the throat. Blossoming up a slender, 3-foot stem, the narrow, tubular corollas — each flaring into five pointed lobes around a cluster of long, delicate, red stamens — will also attract hawkmoths later in the May-to-September season. When not in bloom, skyrocket gilia shows only a basal rosette of narrowly lobed, sticky — and rather smelly — leaves, the reason for its various skunklike monikers.

Regions 2, 4, 5, 6, 7, 8, 9

SKYROCKET GILIA / Gary Ladd

SKYROCKET GILIA / Michael Collier

SKYROCKET GILIA / David W. Lazaroff

Rocky Mountain iris

western blue flag, wild iris
Iris missouriensis
Iris Family

From May to September in Arizona's high country, you can easily spot this perennial's large fleshy flowers of either pale blue or violet — the fragrant blooms measure about 3 inches in diameter and up to 4 inches long. In wet mountain meadows and other damp, high-elevation locales, look for the swordlike bluish green leaves clustered at the base of flower stems, which may grow 2 feet high and bear at least two flowers, sometimes several. The iris is at home in the southeastern mountains up into Regions 7 and 8, ranging from elevations of 6,000 to 9,500 feet. Regions 6, 7, 8, 9

ironwood

desert ironwood, palo de hierro
Olneya tesota
Pea Family

The tree's grayish green leaflets, combined with blossoms varying from deep violet to white, give a pale purplish cast to the washes and slopes where ironwoods live. Ironwoods reach heights of 30 feet and produce one of the heaviest woods in the world. The Seri Indians carve this fine hardwood into polished animal figures. At their range's northern edge, ironwoods freeze often and become more sparse. They seldom extend above 2,500 feet. Bee-pollinated, they have an extremely compact flowering season ranging from three weeks to as few as six days. This season begins in mid-March on the Mexican border, around mid-May farther north or at higher elevations. Regions 1, 2, 3

buckhorn cholla

Opuntia acanthocarpa
Cactus Family

Heavily armed by long spines, each with a sheathlike covering, this forbidding cholla offers dazzling red, yellow, orange, or variegated blossoms. The flowers spiral inward when touched, which douses bees with more pollen. The cactus has joints 6 to 12 inches long and spine-bearing tubercles that are two to three times as long as they are wide. The open, branching habit makes it easy to pick the buds, which are boiled or steamed in pits. Cooked buds have the flavor of asparagus or artichoke. Found from 500 to 3,500 feet, sometimes hybridizing with other chollas, buckhorns are plants of open valleys, desert slopes, and arid canyons. Bloom time runs from mid-April to late May. (Although their common names are similar, the buckhorn is a different species than the staghorn cholla, *Opuntia versicolor*.)

Regions 1, 2, 3, 4

BUCKHORN CHOLLA / Bruce Griffin

BUCKHORN CHOLLA / Randy A. Prentice

BUCKHORN CHOLLA / Larry Ulrich

Engelmann prickly pear

cactus apple, pricklypear, nopal, tuna
Opuntia engelmannii
Cactus Family

The most common prickly pear in Arizona deserts, this species is also one of the most variable. Its branches of pads may be erect, ascending, or sprawling; the joints may be 6 to 10 inches long; and the spines may be flattened, straight, or curved, and colored brown or white. Bees pollinate the flowers, whether colored yellow, pink, or red. It grows from 1,000-foot deserts up to ponderosa-pine and Douglas-fir forests at 7,500 feet. The desert bloom starts around mid-April and wanes in early or mid-June. Relatively reliable in flowering duration, the same individual plants will flower for about the same five or six weeks every year.
Regions 1, 2, 3, 4, 5, 6

blue paloverde

paloverde
Parkinsonia florida
[*Cercidium floridum*]
Pea Family

The blue paloverde is distinguished from the foothills paloverde by larger, fewer leaflets; by all-yellow flower petals with small red spots; and by bark that has a bluer cast. Blue paloverde trees grow more restricted to plains and the margins of dry washes. In most years, the trees bloom very briefly from April to May, but some may bud as early as February or as late as October. Most trees bloom synchronously over a 10-day to three-week period, peaking in late April.
Regions 1, 2, 3

ENGLEMANN PRICKLY PEAR / Larry Ulrich

BLUE PALO VERDE / Les David Manevitz

BLUE PALOVERDE / David W. Lazaroff

FOOTHILLS PALOVERDE / David W. Lazaroff

FOOTHILLS PALOVERDE / Les David Manevitz

foothills paloverde

littleleaf paloverde
Parkinsonia microphylla
[*Cercidium microphyllum*]
Pea Family

This small, green-barked tree of upper desert slopes, or bajadas, has five to seven pairs of leaflets and bicolor (white and yellow) flowers on branches that end in a thornlike point. Its blooming period can be just as brief as that of the blue paloverde; a duration of less than 10 days is not uncommon. This period varies from place to place, but ranges from early March through late May. The pale yellow flowers have white banner petals. During flowering, the yellow of paloverde blossoms can dominate entire desert mountain slopes.

Regions 1, 2, 3, 4, 6

mesquite

velvet mesquite
Prosopis velutina
Pea Family

Perhaps the most common Sonoran Desert tree, mesquite is known nationwide: for its wood, used in fine furniture or as aromatic firewood, and for the mild honey that bees make from its flowers. An average-sized tree produces 12 million flowers per season. This species has slightly curved, often speckled seed pods with sticky beads of sugary sap on them. The pods were the single most important food of Sonoran Desert tribes. The bipinnately compound leaves have 12 to 20 leaflets nearly touching one another. Roots run deep, often reaching underground water. This nitrogen-producing tree starts blooming in late April, wanes by early June, then flowers again in early August. Mesquites are somewhat sensitive to long freezes.

Regions 1, 2, 3, 4, 5, 6

MESQUITE / Dave Bly

MESQUITE / Dave Bly

New Mexico locust

desert locust, New Mexican locust
Robinia neomexicana
Pea Family

From May to July, when this small shrubby tree blooms in its canyon and forest habitats, the heavily dangling clusters of purplish pink blooms almost glow with color against the rock walls and dark conifers surrounding them. Common throughout Arizona up to about 8,500 feet on the North Rim (more rare on the South Rim and in the Grand Canyon itself), New Mexico locusts guard their twigs with paired, half-inch curved spines, but cattle and deer still browse the bluish green, pinnate leaves.

Regions 2, 4, 5, 6, 7, 8, 9

NEW MEXICO LOCUST WITH ASPEN / Jack Dykinga

NEW MEXICO LOCUST / Les David Manevitz

Woods' rose

Arizona rose, wild rose
Rosa woodsii
[*Rosa arizonica*]
Rose Family

Pink and fragrant, the Woods' rose adds a touch of wild romance to ponderosa-pine forests, starting at 4,000 feet in Region 5 and along the Mogollon Rim in Region 7, and up to 9,000 feet in the Kaibab Plateau's white-fir forests. Blooming from May into July, each rose opens five wavy petals around a central cluster of yellow stamens, then the faded petals drop away and leave a small, seedy fruit, or rose hip, to ripen. When full and bright red, rose hips can be eaten as a tart snack, gathered to make a seedy, but tasty jam, or left to attract birds and other wildlife. The branches of pinnate, toothed leaves and quarter-inch thorns can grow into an effective hedge.

Regions 5, 7, 8, 9

WOODS' ROSE / Nick Berezenko

WOODS' ROSE / Suzanne Holden

WOODS' ROSE / Randy A. Prentice

silverleaf nightshade

white horsenettle, trompillo
Solanum elaeagnifolium
Nightshade Family

Striking starlike flowers — violet or bluish violet petals around bright yellow anthers — mark these toxic weeds that bloom from May to October and then follow with small yellow berries. Growing to 3 feet tall along roadsides and fields between elevations of 1,000 and 5,000 feet, this perennial carries silvery oblong leaves with wavy edges and spiny undersides.

Regions 1, 2, 3, 4, 5, 6, 7, 8, 9

SILVERLEAF NIGHTSHADE / Randy A. Prentice

PRINCE'S PLUME / Gary Ladd

PRINCE'S PLUME / Michael Collier

PRINCE'S PLUME / Chuck Lawsen

desert prince's plume

golden prince's-plume,
princesplume
Stanleya pinnata
Mustard Family

A spectacular desert mustard that can reach 6 feet high, this spiky, woody-based perennial blooms from May to September over dry plains and mesas between 2,500 and 6,000 feet and in the Grand Canyon. The elongated yellow blooms with their exaggerated stamens look like feathers as they flower progressively up the stalks.

Regions 3, 4, 5, 7, 8, 9

yellow trumpetbush

Arizona yellow bells,
trumpetflower
Tecoma stans
Bignonia Family

A multi-stemmed shrub with shiny leaves divided into five arrow-shaped leaflets, yellow trumpetbush showers the landscape with golden flowers much of the year. In frost-free areas, they grow into a large tree. The roots are still used medicinally in Mexico. The yellow trumpetbush prefers dry, rocky, or gravelly slopes below 5,500 feet in deserts or in grasslands and woodland canyons which drain into deserts. The flower's sensitive stigma slams shut like a clam when touched. The shrub begins to bloom and attract large bees in late April, flowering sporadically into November or December.
Regions 2, 6

American speedwell

brooklime
Veronica americana
Figwort Family

A semi-aquatic plant, speedwell spreads its stems along mountain streams and springs between elevations of 1,500 to 9,500 feet. Broad, dark green leaves frame the blue lavender, four-lobed flowers that bloom, from May through August, in clusters staggered up the stems.
Regions 3, 5, 7, 9

YELLOW TRUMPETBUSH / Bruce Griffin

AMERICAN SPEEDWELL / Suzanne Holden

AMERICAN SPEEDWELL / Suzanne Holden

SOAPTREE YUCCA / Bruce Griffin

SOAPTREE YUCCA / Dave Bly

ROCKY MOUNTAIN ZINNIA / Bruce Griffin

soaptree yucca

soapweed yucca, izote forrajero
Yucca elata
Agave Family

A tall, multi-branched yucca, the soaptree has narrow leaves with threadlike margins and dry capsules that split open and disperse their seeds on the wind. The creamy white flowers grow on long stalks. They are pollinated by specialized moths. Soaptree roots historically were used as a shampoo, and Indians have woven its leaves into baskets throughout time. A grassland species, soaptree yucca extends farther into the Chihuahuan Desert than into the Sonoran Desert. It blooms in June and July in southern Arizona and in early April and May at lower elevations in central Arizona.
Regions 1, 2, 5, 6, 9

Rocky Mountain zinnia

plains zinnia, desert zinnia
Zinnia grandiflora
Sunflower Family

A low perennial with clusters of bright yellow flowers, the Rocky Mountain zinnia is a warm-season bloomer. Its opposite, three-ribbed leaves underlay a profusion of blooms from May through October. Its pollen attracts a considerable number of honeybees from August onward. This species grows in grasslands and oak woodlands, but does well when cultivated in the desert. Preferring elevations between 4,000 and 6,500 feet, it grows on semi-arid slopes, mesas, and plains.
Regions 2, 4, 5, 6, 7

6 AFTER THE STORMS
Summer & Fall

During midsummer's long, hot days, fat-bellied clouds build up over the Sonoran and Chihuahuan deserts. Moist air currents from Mexico sweep up into Arizona, seeding the thunderclouds that surge in, pushing dust storms and violent lightning before them.

Popularly called "monsoons," the resulting hard, brief rains churn up dormant seeds, which start germinating in the hot, drenched surface layers of soil. A new set of plants emerges within days, even hours, of those first summer rains, which are heavy enough to send flash floods coursing down desert washes.

The summer wildflowers seldom appear as one large sweep of color. Most bloom in a scatter and become concentrated only along the edges of roads and washes, like the showy stands of Rocky Mountain beeplant in the northern regions.

The shorter growing seasons in Regions 5, 7, 8, and 9 mean that flowering plants must start winding down their blooms and readying fruits and seeds to ripen and disperse before winter hits. First frosts and snowfalls can come as early as September in the higher elevations of Regions 7 and 9.

Arranged in alphabetical order by scientific name, the individual plant descriptions list a primary common name in bold, some alternate common names, the scientific name (genus and species) in italics, and the plant's family name. (See page 7 for the taxonomic standard.)

WEST OF ARIVACA JUNCTION, ARIZONA CALTROPS VIE WITH INTRODUCED MORNING GLORY FLOWERS.
Randy A. Prentice

century plant

Parry's agave, mescal
Agave parryi
Agave Family

This century plant takes more than 25 years to send up its 12- to 18-foot flowering stalk, bloom, and then die. Its wide, spatula-shaped leaves make compact heads with a pale gray green cast to them. Yellow stamens protruding from the pale flowers brighten the subdued grasslands and woodlands. Although bats pollinate other large-panicled agaves, this species extends beyond the range of nectar-feeding bats and may be pollinated by bees and hummingbirds. The species ranges to 9,000 feet in elevation, suggesting considerable freeze tolerance. It blooms mid-June to mid-August, with entire clonal populations flowering synchronously. Regions 5, 6

CENTURY PLANT / Stewart Aitchison

CENTURY PLANT / Paul Gill

CENTURY PLANT / Randy A. Prentice

saiya

Mexican yellowshow, throwup
weed, saya, zaya, temaqui
Amoreuxia palmatifida
Lipstick Tree Family

These herbs rise, after the summer rains, from a perennial tuberous rootstock and persist above ground less than three months. The orange flowers cluster above or between hand-shaped leaves. Lacking nectar but still showy, the five petals have brown spots at their bases and numerous stamens, which drop their pollen when bees buzz or vibrate their wings nearby. Every part of the plant is edible, from parsnip-like roots to seed capsules, which are used as a coffee substitute. Found in hills and canyons from 3,000 to 6,000 feet, it flowers July through September. Regions 2, 3, 6

showy milkweed

Asclepias speciosa
Milkweed Family

The strikingly large, coarse leaves have a slight sheen on top and white hairs furring their undersides. Upright stalks, often topping 3 feet in height, support large puffball clusters of starry flowers, each flower with five rose purple sepals, five narrowly pointed lavender pink petals, and five lavender pink horned hoods. A perennial named for its milky sap, the showy milkweed flowers from June into August, then the woolly hornlike pods ripen and fill with tiny seeds bearing a silky floss that will carry them on the wind. One of several Arizona milkweed species, it grows at elevations from 6,000 to 9,000 feet in conifer forest clearings, along roadsides, and in seasonally moist areas. Regions 7, 8

SAIYA / Bruce Griffin

SHOWY MILKWEED / Suzanne Holden

fernbush

desert-sweet, tansy bush
Chamaebatiaria millefolium
Rose Family

Just as its common names imply, the fernbush's finely cut, compound leaves are fernlike, quite aromatic, and eye-catching even without the 4-inch-long panicles of striking white flowers. The flowers — five crinkly petals surrounding yellow stamens — hang from the branch ends during August and September. Both the grayish green leaves and the half-inch flowers exude a certain stickiness. Fernbush is common in the Grand Canyon, on the South Rim, and on the North Rim up to 8,000 feet. In woodland, scrub, and forest communities at elevations down to 4,500 feet, fernbush may even bloom into early November.
Regions 4, 5, 7, 8, 9

Rocky Mountain beeplant

bee spiderflower, stinking clover, pink cleome
Cleome serrulata
Caper Family

This spiky, 3-foot-tall annual blooms throughout fields, roadsides, and foothills of the central highlands up to elevations of 7,000 feet. The half-inch-long flowers — four petals shading from pale pink to purple around long delicate stamens tipped with green anthers — cluster at the head of the stem in an eye-catching raceme, 3 to 5 inches long and up to 3 inches wide. They bloom during the late summer. The skinny, palmately compound leaflets are eclipsed by the flowers that later give way to long, thin seedpods.
Regions 5, 7, 9

FERNBUSH / Suzanne Holden

ROCKY MOUNTAIN BEEPLANT / Larry Ulrich

ROCKY MOUNTAIN BEEPLANT / Tom Bean

BIRD-BILL DAYFLOWER / Suzanne Holden

BIRD-BILL DAYFLOWER / Suzanne Holden

FINGERLEAF GOURD / Tanya Beth Kinsey

bird-bill dayflower

birdbill dayflower, western dayflower
Commelina dianthifolia
Spiderwort Family

Three petals of startling blue last for barely a single summer day, sometimes even wilting by midafternoon, which is how this grasslike perennial got its name. Long, narrow, deeply creased leaves sheath the tall, upright stems, which support several blooms during the flowering season, August to September. Forming a rounded triangle — two above, a slightly smaller one below — the broadly lobed petals frame six golden stamens, all cupped in a thin, boat-shaped bract that juts from the stem at almost a right angle. Dayflowers grow in pine and mixed conifer forests between 3,500 and 9,500 feet.
Regions 2, 5, 6, 7, 8

fingerleaf gourd

coyote gourd, chichicayota
Cucurbita digitata
Gourd Family

This warm-season vine emerges prior to summer rains from huge water-storing taproots. One form, with fingerlike lobed leaves, hybridizes with a broader leaved form found from the Yuma area westward into California. The large, pale yellow flowers open before dawn and are pollinated by at least two kinds of squash and gourd bees. Both male and female bees visit these flowers, the males patrolling for mates and sleeping in the flowers while they are closed for the night. Blooms are followed by large, round, green-striped or yellow gourds. The roots and gourds have been used medicinally for millennia. Flowering time occurs as early as May and as late as October.
Regions 1, 2, 3, 4, 5, 6

FIREWEED / Paul Gill

CORAL BEAN / Dave Bly

CORAL BEAN / Randy A. Prentice

fireweed

blooming sally, willow weed, willowherb
Epilobium angustifolium ssp. *angustifolium*
Evening Primrose Family

These spikes of late-summer color, sometimes 6 feet tall, bloom from July to September along roads and on the disturbed soil of logged forests and forest fire burns (therefore the common name). Colored a deep rose purple and slightly ruffled, the four petals splay wide around long, pale stamens and form long racemes atop the leggy stems and narrow leaves. Look for fireweed in damp mountain habitats, from elevations of 7,000 to 11,500 feet.
Regions 6, 7, 9

coral bean

coralbean, patol
Erythrina flabelliformis
Pea Family

Coral beans are peculiar among the Arizona flora in that they begin to bloom before their shiny, aspen-like leaves appear on the short, woody branches. These shrubs begin to bloom in early June, peaking two to three weeks later and terminating completely by late July. Leaves and red-beaned pods begin to develop as the summer rains come, but the leaves seldom persist more than two months. Black-chinned hummingbirds are among the pollinators of the sucrose-rich tubular flowers. The blood-red seeds are rich in toxic alkaloids, which, along with ants, partially protect the seeds from consumption by moth larvae. Coral bean is found from 3,000 to 5,000 feet in desert grasslands and oak-pine woodlands.
Regions 2, 3, 6

DEER EARS / Tom Bean

DEER EARS / Nick Berezenko

deer ears

monument plant, deers ears, elkweed, green gentian
Frasera speciosa
[*Swertia radiata*]
Gentian Family

There are flowers with brighter colors than this gentian's pale whitish green, but the lobed petals' purple streaking and stippling add a touch of unrivaled glamour to a monumental flower stalk. Blooming from about June (sometimes as early as May) to August or September, the starlike flowers (as many as 600 per plant) cluster around the length of the towering stem, which can loom up to 6 feet tall. Broad, smooth, oblong leaves splay in a large rosette at the base of the stalk, while smaller, narrower leaves spiral up the stem and jut out from among the flowers. Stands of deer ears grow in moist pine-forest meadows and aspen/pine forests between 5,000 and 10,000 feet, including both rims of the Grand Canyon.

Regions 2, 5, 6, 7, 8, 9

BARREL CACTUS / Suzanne Holden

BARREL CACTUS / Suzanne Holden

WILD COTTON / Tanya Beth Kinsey

barrel cactus

fishhook barrel, Wislizenus' barrel
Ferocactus wislizenii
Cactus Family

This rotund cactus has dark, hooked, flattened spines with bristles between them. It is one of the taller species of barrel cactus. While it can store much liquid in its succulent flesh, it responds rapidly after a rain, immediately putting out new root hairs to capture new soil moisture. It blooms with the summer rains, beginning by mid-June and peaking in late August. Cup-shaped flowers may range from red to yellow, but most are orange. The flowers open mid-morning and have little fragrance, but attract many bees, and ultimately produce delicious yellow fruit. Regions 1, 2, 5, 6

wild cotton

Thurber's cotton, desert cotton
Gossypium thurberi
Mallow Family

Since this relative of cultivated cotton also serves as an alternate host for the boll weevil, farmers often remove it from nearby fields. Yet its lovely five-lobed leaves and pale pink to whitish flowers justify its protection for ornamental value where it grows apart from cotton fields. Many bees and wasps are attracted to its floral nectar, but it also exudes nectar on the leaves and flower stalks, thereby attracting other insects. Preferring rocky slopes and washes, it ranges from high desert at 2,500 feet to oak and juniper woodland at 5,000 feet. It is known to flower as early as April, but most blooming and fruiting occurs from August to October. Regions 1, 2, 3, 6

ORANGE SNEEZEWEED / Paul Gill

DESERT ROSEMALLOW / Tanya Beth Kinsey

ORANGE SNEEZEWEED / Michael Collier

desert rosemallow Coulter hibiscus, pelotazo *Hibiscus coulteri* Mallow Family	The spectacular mix of colors in the large flowers of this straggling shrub can stop any hiker dead in his tracks. Each delicate yellow petal has a blood-red basal spot amidst other markings. Many kinds of bees find this flower attractive, although certain species specialize in the mallow group. Its slender, woody branches reach 4 feet high, but it never develops a large canopy. Desert rosemallow blooms sporadically throughout the year, even during late fall-early winter droughts. It inhabits steep canyons from 1,500 to 4,500 feet in desert and desert grassland. Regions 1, 2, 3, 5, 6
orange sneezeweed owl's claws, owlsclaws, western sneezeweed *Hymenoxys hoopesii* [*Dulgaldia hoopesii*] or [*Helenium hoopesii*] Sunflower Family	A constant source of color from June to September, this rather frowsy sunflower blooms profusely in conifer forests and high mountain meadows at elevations between 7,000 and 10,000 feet. Sneezeweed often grows in dense stands, sometimes coloring a whole field golden when each plant's multiple woolly stems branch and bear the daisylike flowers. Skinny and pointed, the golden to orange yellow ray flowers unevenly surround a central, darker yellow disk. On older blooms, the ray flowers start to droop and curve back from the center. The large, woolly, grayish green leaves grow at an upright angle from the base of the plant, which can average a 3-foot height. Regions 2, 6, 7, 8, 9

Arizona caltrop

orange caltrop, summer-poppy, Arizona poppy
Kallstroemia grandiflora
Caltrop Family

This summer bloomer has five orange petals, each with pale red veins. A ground-creeping herb with divided leaves, it has numerous flowers, which bloom simultaneously. It germinates with the first summer rains, then sprawls out in wet pockets along roads and washes to cover whole patches with luxuriant growth. Quick to bloom once established, its desert and grassland flowering season may extend from early July through October, but most years it lasts only from late July to mid-September. Bees accidentally pollinate this plant when they groom themselves of its sticky pollen.

Regions 1, 2, 3, 5, 6

ARIZONA CALTROP / Suzanne Holden

ARIZONA CALTROP / Randy Prentice

cardinal flower

scarlet lobelia
Lobelia cardinalis
Bellflower Family

Although found throughout generally arid elevations of about 3,000 to 7,500 feet, this 2-foot- to 3-foot-tall herbaceous perennial lives where it finds moisture. Look for the upright stems and long, narrow, dark green leaves along streams, springs, seeps, and moist meadows. The spikes of scarlet flowers attract hummingbirds and butterflies from June into October. Bees also pollinate the tubular blooms, which flare open into two lips. The upper lip has two narrow upright lobes, while the larger lower lip flamboyantly extends into three deeply cut points.

June through October

Regions 1, 2, 3, 4, 5, 6, 7, 8, 9

CARDINAL FLOWER / Gary Ladd

CARDINAL FLOWER / Ralph Lee Hopkins

pincushion cactus

fishhook cactus, fishhook pincushion
Mammillaria grahamii var. *grahamii*
Cactus Family

The small, cylindrical stems of this cactus produce pink to lavender blooms with white margins, which are pollinated by bees. The scarlet, berry-like fruit that follow are as colorful as the flowers themselves. Although their hooked central spines offer some protection against browsers, this species tends to grow beneath chain fruit cholla, thereby avoiding animal feeding and trampling. Stems are often solitary, or sometimes in small clusters. It is common on both heavy and light soils, on rocky slopes and plains of deserts, and grasslands below 4,500 feet. Its flowering range is from mid-April through early September, but it appears to be triggered by summer rains, putting out new flowers five to seven days after each drenching.
Regions 1, 2, 3, 4, 5

Franciscan bluebells

Mertensia franciscana
Borage Family

These dainty blue flowers like the moist, shaded forests of the conifer and aspen belts, so they grow mostly above 7,000 feet, including the Grand Canyon's North Rim. The pendulous clusters of tubular flowers, shading from dark blue to pale blue (sometimes even including white or pinkish blooms), swing against shiny, dark green, narrowly pointed leaves from June to September.
Regions 2, 6, 7, 9

PINCUSHION CACTUS / Jack Dykinga

PINCUSHION CACTUS / Suzanne Holden

FRANCISCAN BLUEBELLS / Bruce Griffin

wild bergamot

horsemint, bee balm
Monarda fistulosa var.
menthifolia
Mint Family

Crush the aromatic, purple-tinged foliage, and you'll recognize this perennial's mint family ties. Lavender pink tubular flowers, fringed with stamens extending beyond the two curved lips, top the branches like tassels. The toothed, lance-shaped leaves extend up to 2 3/4 inches from square, purplish stems. Look for bergamot to bloom all summer along high-country roadsides and in moist pine and spruce-fir forests between 5,000 and 9,000 feet.

Regions 5, 7, 9

WILD BERGAMOT / Larry Lindahl

WILD BERGAMOT / Larry Lindahl

JUMPING CHOLLA / Larry Ulrich

JUMPING CHOLLA / Bruce Griffin

jumping cholla

chain fruit cholla, cholla brillante
Opuntia fulgida
Cactus Family

A tall, thick-stemmed cholla, this species lacks the knob-like tubercles on its fruit that are present in most other chollas. Its long, spiny, inch-thick joints are readily detachable with the slightest pressure, hence their apparent "jumping" nature. The small, bee-pollinated flowers are deep pink. Flowers and fruit tend to hang upside-down from pendant branches of this tree-like cactus. Flowering runs from the dryness of mid-May, through the mid-summer rains, into late August. The peak is between late July and early August. Below 4,000 feet, jumping chollas cover a wide range of habitats but form impenetrable stands along the U.S.-Mexican border west of Organ Pipe Cactus National Monument. Regions 1, 2, 3

night-blooming cereus

reina-de-la-noche, Arizona queen-of-the-night
Peniocereus greggii
[*Cereus greggii*]
Cactus Family

The waxy-white, 6-inch-long flowers of this tuberous cactus produce a fragrance that can be smelled 100 feet away. Beginning just after dusk, during June and July, the buds unfold quickly, in spasms, to attract moths and other insects throughout the night and until dawn. On a single plant, anywhere from one flower to 25 flowers can open in the same night, but rarely does a plant's total floral production exceed 50 blossoms per year. The flowers are produced on slender, lead-colored stems that often camouflage themselves under creosote bushes. Regions 1, 2, 3, 6

NIGHT-BLOOMING CEREUS / Jack Dykinga

NIGHT-BLOOMING CEREUS / Dave Bly

scarlet cinquefoil

red cinquefoil
Potentilla thurberi
Rose Family

Spreading handlike into five or seven leaflets with finely toothed edges, the dark green leaves may be 2 inches long at the base and smaller along the stem. The cupped, dark red flowers nod at the top of the stems, which sometimes grow 16 inches high. A hit with bees, this summer bloomer flowers July through October in high-country conifer forests from 6,000 to 9,000 feet.

Regions 3, 5, 6, 7, 8

devil's claw

unicorn plant, devilsclaw, doubleclaw
Proboscidea parviflora
Unicorn Plant Family

Amid this annual's long, sprawling stems and large, sticky, arrow-shaped leaves, the velvety, five-lobed flowers wait for certain large bees. Once inside a reddish purple, pink, and yellow-striped tubular flower, a bee will trigger the sensitive stigma to "slam shut" after pollination. The green, okra-like fruit matures, sloughs off its skin, splits down the middle, and two woody, horn-like projections curl back. Southwestern Indians domesticated a variety with unusually long horns and still use the horn fibers to decorate their basketry. On wet roadsides or in washes, devil's claw will sometimes flower in mid-May, but most don't even germinate until the summer rains and then start flowering within three weeks. This second flush may last from mid-July through mid-October. Centuries of Indian trade and agriculture have spread devil's claw to a range now stretching from 500 to 5,000 feet.

Regions 1, 2, 3, 4, 5, 6

SCARLET CINQUEFOIL / Marty Cordano

DEVIL'S CLAW / George H. H. Huey

NEW MEXICAN CHECKER MALLOW / Michael Collier

MEXICAN CAMPION / Jerry Sieve

New Mexican checkermallow

salt spring checkerbloom, alkali pink
Sidalcea neomexicana
Mallow Family

Despite a deep taproot, this thirsty, high-country perennial prefers regular moisture and will go dormant during dry periods. With a steady water supply — along streams or seeps or in moist meadows, at elevations between 5,000 and 9,500 feet — the checkermallow will bloom, June through September. Tightly furled buds angle up the slender, wandlike stems. Then, shaded deep pink to purple, each flower's five notched petals will open around a central set of stamens. After the first summer flush, a spate of late rains can induce a repeat bloom. The large lobed leaves at the plant's base have rounded, scalloped edges, while the smaller, upper leaves have deep palmate divisions.
Regions 2, 5, 6, 7, 8, 9

Mexican campion

cardinal catchfly, Indian pink
Silene laciniata
Pink Family

A bright spot of red in pine forests of the high country, 5,500 to 9,000 feet up, this perennial blooms from July to October. The rather spindly plants bear their festive, cardinal red blooms on upright, narrow stems set with alternating pairs of narrow, sticky leaves. Each slender, tubular flower spreads into five deeply fringed, or "pinked," petals.
Regions 2, 5, 6, 7, 9

false hellebore

corn lily, skunk cabbage
Veratrum californicum
Lily Family

The whitish green stars of individual flowers, closely arrayed on long, branching clusters, are not inconspicuous during July and August. Still, when driving by a mountain meadow, you'll first see the broad, strongly veined, upright, 1-foot-long leaves clasping the stout stems in whorls. The roots and young shoots are extremely toxic to livestock, and the flowers are just as fatal to bees and other insects. These striking plants grow where there is plenty of water: in bogs and wet meadows at elevations of 7,500 to 9,500 feet.

Regions 5, 6, 7

FALSE HELLEBORE / Jack Dykinga

common mullein

flannel plant, velvet dock
Verbascum thapsus
Figwort Family

Introduced from Europe in colonial times, mullein — its tightly packed spike of yellow, lobed flowers rising on a tall, wooly stalk above a rosette of big, felted leaves — shows up in this book because of the plant's high visibility along roadsides, fields, and railroad embankments throughout the West. Like another introduced foreigner, the tumbleweed (originally from Russia), mullein became an integral part of our wild landscape. This biennial flowers the entire summer, June into October, at elevations of 4,500 to 8,000 feet. Sometimes 6 feet tall, the stalks line dry highway shoulders and open forest areas throughout Arizona, from the Chiricahua Mountains to the both rims of the Grand Canyon.
Regions 1, 2, 3, 4, 5, 6, 7, 8, 9

COMMON MULLEIN / Tom Danielsen

COMMON MULLEIN / George H. H. Huey

BADLANDS MULE'S EARS / Gary Ladd

MOUNTAIN DEATHCAMAS / Suzanne Holden

badlands mule's ears

rough mules ears
Wyethia scabra
Sunflower Family

Distinctively rough to the touch and finely toothed on the edges, this perennial's narrow, pointed leaves look a bit scrubby next to the lush, much larger leaves of its highly visible cousin, the Arizona mule's ears (*Wyethia arizonica*) of the high pine forests. But badlands mule's ears adds its own robust dash of color along the dry slopes and sandy mesas (between 5,000 and 6,000 feet) where it grows. From June to October, the plant's several stiff, hairy stems, clumped together at a woody base and up to 30 inches tall, will bear large flowerheads of bright yellow ray flowers encircling a mass of yellow to yellowish brown disk flowers. Regions 7, 8

mountain deathcamas

white camas, wand lily, alkali grass
Zigadenus elegans
Lily Family

Found growing in rich-soiled grasslands, pine woods, and damp rocky niches between elevations of 5,000 and 10,000 feet, including the Grand Canyon's North Rim, this toxic plant's small bulb first sprouts a set of grasslike leaves. Then it sends up a bare stem to support a raceme of bell-shaped flowers. Blooming during July and August, the greenish or yellowish white flowers are slightly tinged with purple. Regions 6, 7, 9

CAPTURING THE MAGIC
Growing Wildflowers at Home

If you've ever wandered through a yard devoted to native annual wildflowers, trees, and shrubs, you may have walked away with a sense of harmony. The setting is in synch with the underlying nature of its surroundings. That compatibility is often forgotten in a lavish but contrived urban landscape, a Mediterranean-flavored suburban subdivision, or even in a single-crop farm.

The native setting has the color, the fragrance, and sometimes the wildlife that could be found on the same site a hundred or even a thousand years ago. Such native plantings soon become less of another human contrivance and more a blending with natural settings much larger and older than all of us. Having native wildflowers around our home reminds us of the uniqueness of our local setting and makes that distinctive sense of place part of our lives.

Certain natives require less water and less pampering than commonplace exotics. Since outdoor uses account for more than half the water consumed in southwestern cities, such excesses should hardly be tolerated in a region where this resource is already limited.

When we actively show appreciation for native plant life, rather than overlooking it, we are recognizing its value to our everyday lives, thereby encouraging its conservation in its wild setting. As desert ecologist Paul Sears observed many decades ago, "People seldom try to save anything that they haven't yet learned to love." By becoming familiar with native plants in general, we may be more likely to protect particular rare ones threatened by our own activities.

Planting and nurturing wildflowers can be a tangible pleasure. We can watch a dozen kinds of wildflowers sprout, bloom, and seed within a few feet of where we eat and sleep, tying our lives into the soil and seasonal changes.

Nurseries and seed catalogs now make more and more native seeds and plants commercially available and much new information has emerged regarding their care and feeding. It is easier than ever before to return our gardens to the natives or to heighten the beauty of a yard where natural vegetation already exists.

Perhaps the most important preparation for a wildflower garden is in matching the site you choose with the wildflower array suited to your area.

AN ARES METALMARK BUTTERFLY PERCHES ON A DESERT MARIGOLD.
Bruce Griffin

Get to know the various parts of your yard from a wildflower's point of view. What is growing on it now, and how well do these plants fare over different patches of soil? What do old-timers or historic descriptions of your town say about what grew on it in decades past? How well does the ground hold moisture? Is the soil surface slick after a rain but quick to dry again? Is there much runoff? Does caliche hardpan limit deep root growth? How much of the day does sunshine reach one spot versus

another? Does frost hit one side of the yard harder than the rest? Once you have discovered the microenvironments in your own yard, you will begin to notice wild plants that comfortably grow under natural conditions not unlike the topographic niches in your yard. Using this book and others, keep a checklist of natives potentially suited to your own setting. Walk around the vacant lots, desert washes, or open lands nearest to your home.

What wild species do well there that can be added to your own site? (If neighbors want to share seed from wildflowers volunteering on their own land, this may be just as good a source as any.) You may not necessarily want all future plantings to adapt to your lot as it is. Maybe it is worth terracing an eroding hillside, or digging out old building rubble and refuse from a trash pit, building up fertile organic matter in their stead. For the calcium-carbonate hardpan known as caliche, you may even want to rent a jackhammer or soil auger to crack through subsurface layers in order to give tree and shrub roots more room to grow. Removing Bermuda grass may also be necessary, and can be done either by physical or chemical means.

How do you use your yard? Yards seldom function solely for aesthetic pleasure. Both native and non-native plantings may get in the way of certain activities if inappropriately located or improperly maintained. Newcomers to Arizona naively dismiss native plants as being incompatible with family life around the yard, even though exotics (introduced ornamentals) may be just as incongruous in some settings. It's true that you don't want to plant prickly pear in the midst of where the kids play football, but neither will you want to plant the spiny, non-native pyracantha. On the other hand, native grama grasses and touch football may make a great team.

If you don't need to reserve space for an occasional ballgame or have no predilection for formal garden plantings but love birds and flowers, you may opt for a more natural planting design.

In the northern United States, these have been collectively termed wildflower meadows, whether they are tall-grass prairies replacing trimmed lawns or bog gardens modeled after the flora of primeval wetlands. The goal is a mix of plants blooming at different times of the year that replicates a natural habitat of the region in terms of life forms, plant spacing, and diversity.

This naturalistic approach is a reasonable way to treat areas that are still relatively untouched or to enhance lots with just remnants of the preexisting vegetation, complementing these with formerly present species. You simply weave colorful species back into the slightly worn fabric of Nature's quilt work. For instance, reintroduced wildflowers can be sown beneath the canopy of taller mesquites and clusters of cactus or subshrubs planted nearby.

Yet it is a fallacy to consider native plants as being suitable only in such wild settings.

As author Jill Nokes wrote in her horticultural guide, *How to Grow Native Plants of Texas and the Southwest*: "Because few people want the thicket or wild look in their yards, they believe they must forgo native plants altogether. . . But native plants can and should be used as single specimen plants, formal hedges, or ground covers . . . or as perennials mixed with other exotic bedding plants."

Nokes' observation holds true in many formal landscape designs scattered throughout the Southwest and northern Mexico. Clusters of yellow flowers on trumpetbush shrubs are pruned into beautiful courtyard carousels in Baja California. Large agaves or stocky barrel cacti, set into volcanic rocks and cinders and angled in different directions, make elegant, sculpture-like focal points in plazas. Hedgerows of Joshua tree, prickly pear, or sotol can add much more texture to a home landscape than can a row of non-native oleander or privet.

Even when a family opts for a formal patio or porch, planters and beds full of native annual wildflowers can offer life that overused pink petunias can't come close to. Overall, it is best to think of how you want a flower bed, windbreak, sound barrier, or sidewalk margin to function, then scan the wide range of natives and select one for the job. In many cases, there is an indigenous plant that can fit the bill once you decide what color, size, and shape you want.

Once you find a source of seed or nursery stock, it is best to read the detailed planting descriptions provided by the supplier. Sometimes, a California strain of a native wildflower sold in Arizona may bloom at a somewhat different time than the usual blooming period of an Arizona strain.

Many beautifully flowering trees, herbs, cacti, and shrubs are available from Arizona nurseries and at botanical garden and arboretum plant sales. The native nursery stock found for sale is often at least a year old, providing a head start over what you could get by planting seeds. When buying such plants, select ones with healthy foliage and, if visible, root systems that do not appear pot-bound or knotted. A vigorous-looking plant can be easily transported and stored until you have prepared a hole for its transplanting.

Choose a site where the plant can mature without growing up into the canopy of nearby trees and where its roots will not compete too fiercely with others. If it loves sun, make sure that it will not find itself shaded by a faster-growing plant after a few years. If you do not want it to impinge on other plants, imagine how high and wide it will grow ultimately and judge how much shade it will cast then.

If you do want to plant from seed and are thinking of collecting wild seed on your own, remember that it may be done legally only if you have written permission from the managing agency (for plants on public lands)

A FIELD OF NON-NATIVE DAISIES IN THE WHITE MOUNTAINS UPSTAGE A DISTANT CLUSTER OF ORANGE SNEEZEWEED.
Jack Dykinga

or from the private land owner. Besides such legal obligations, of course we have the natural obligation to the ecosystem: A wild stand of flowers needs to be able to adequately reseed to provide for new plants in the future. Most of us, of course, have no way of knowing how to judge if we have collected too much seed or even if we've accidentally "robbed" the reproductive future from a threatened species. For flowers that may not be widely available from large commercial nurseries, Arizona's botanical gardens again are an excellent source for native seeds.

When shopping for seeds, you may find premixed regional wildflower seed packets, but their quality varies greatly from one company to another. Gardeners trying them for the first time should not expect too much. Premixed packets marketed for certain regions often are so general that perhaps only one or two species will be compatible with your locale. Many Southwestern mixes combine species from several, sometimes incompatible, climatic regions throughout Arizona and neighboring states; seeds in such generalized mixes truly are Southwestern, but only a fraction are suited to grow successfully in any one specific area. You may also find that these mixes tend to lump together plants that flower in different seasons. Planting them at the same time, you may be able to enjoy successive blooms, due to season, but you may also find that some seeds were planted too early or too late to thrive, mature, and bloom. Also, some poorer quality regional mixes contain a high percentage of introduced weeds. It is safer and more creative, though less convenient and maybe a little more costly, to buy seed packets of plants that will grow in your area, and then mix your own array of wildflowers for a particular bed and a particular season.

Not all the seeds you plant the first year will come up in that season, so plan to use that bed for the same mix over several years' time. Different species of wildflowers have different sets of germination inhibitors that a natural set of circumstances would take care of normally. Some seeds need a flash flood to soften them for germination, in which case you may need to scarify or abrade them before planting. For some, an overnight soaking may do the trick, for others the trigger lies in how they respond to light conditions: simulating seasonal changes by keeping them tucked away in a dry closet for a time and then exposing them to light. Such details you usually can learn from the source for your native seeds or plants.

A loose, crumbly soil is best for encouraging seed germination. Soil that is uncompacted, or perhaps previously worked, is preferable. In any case, the ground should be machine-tilled or shovel-dug to 8 or 9 inches deep. This should be done one or two months before planting.

In opening the ground, you risk the danger of competition from weeds. If noxious weeds have grown on the site in years past, you should reduce their seed reserve in the soil and learn what their seedlings look like before you open the same ground to your wildflower friends. Water the area, letting these weed seeds sprout, then remove the weed seedlings once or twice before planting wildflowers. For small areas, manual removal of weeds is sufficient, but professionals often rely on a mix of mechanical removal and herbicides — either pre-emergent chemicals targeted at certain weedy species, or post-emergent general herbicides. If you are considering using herbicides, keep in mind that certain chemicals also kill desirable plants, so take steps to minimize impact to them, as well as to human health and to wildlife.

A FIELD ALONG THE MOGOLLON RIM'S CHEVELON CREEK GROWS HIGH WITH PINK WILD BERGAMOT, YELLOW CUTLEAF CONEFLOWER, AND BLUE LARKSPUR.
Nick Berezenko

Sprinkling the planting bed with water once or twice before seeding or transplanting also gives you a chance to test the soil's water-holding and infiltration capacity. If it is a heavy clay soil, till in a 1-inch layer of sand. Adding 2 or 3 inches of organic matter, in the form of compost or peat, may also be helpful in increasing soil's water-holding capacity for a small bed, but this may be too costly and generally inappropriate for extensive desert landscaping. For zones where the local soil is mainly decomposed granite — around Prescott and Flagstaff, for instance — regularly working in organic matter, like grass clippings and kitchen compost, will benefit your plants.

Although many competent horticulturalists recommend manure and nitrogen fertilizers for wildflowers, research suggests that such treatment may be unnecessary or even harmful for some wildflowers. For one thing, some nitrogen fertilizers may encourage prolonged leafy growth at the expense of early flowering. Ammonium phosphate or other high phosphorus fertilizers may actually encourage flowering more than those with high nitrogen to phosphorus ratios.

Second, inorganic nitrogen inhibits several kinds of beneficial soil microorganisms that coexist with plant roots, and so such fertilizer reduces the benefits that these microbes provide for plant growth and survival.

Finally, one attraction of native plants is that often they do not need extensive maintenance, like fertilization, since they have adapted to local soils, which are sometimes nutrient-poor and highly alkaline.

For more step-by-step gardening guidelines, see the fine resources at the end of this chapter. The Desert Botanical Garden's Plant Questions Hotline, (480) 941-1225, is available to help desert gardeners on weekdays, 10 to 11:30 A.M. Several municipal agencies in Arizona provide workshops on using native plants for water-wise landscaping, and local nurseries are increasingly helpful resources on growing native plants.

Obviously, in the wild, most plants survive on rainfall, without supplemental irrigation. However, many of these wild plants initially establish themselves during unusually wet years or may require several consecutive wet years. Other plants grow only where storm runoff collects and the soil stays moist much longer than on the surrounding desert slopes. Planted densely, desert natives do require regular watering.

In fact, many herbs and shrubs have growth rates directly proportional to the amount of water supplied them: They will use water if it is provided, but can survive on less if they must. The key factor for making their drought adaptations work for you is to water these natives on need, irrigating the area slowly and deeply. This encourages their roots to grow wider and deeper, gaining soil moisture not touched by superficial evaporation from the surface.

Once healthy roots are established, your plants will need to be watered

LIKE A HUMMINGBIRD, A HAWKMOTH HOVERS NEAR A WILD BERGAMOT FLOWER. Tom Danielsen

less frequently and can endure on their own during extended periods when you are on vacation or otherwise away from home. Mature trees such as mesquite, paloverde, prickly pear cactus, and yucca can survive on their own with little or no supplemental water.

Overall, native plants require no more maintenance than ones of other origin. It may be necessary to trim back the dried, dead stalks of desert ephemeral wildflowers after the season is over, but this holds true for other bedding plants as well. Pruning is necessary for straggly branches of native mesquite as much as it is for those of introduced mulberry or citrus trees. Dried-up annual wildflowers can be pulled up, shaken over the bed to release any seeds, and composted.

With your annual wildflowers well established, you may still wish to reseed annually for two to three years to build up a large seed load in the soil.

Enjoy your successes. Note the time of germination and flowering on a calendar. The duration and intensity will be different each year.

Besides the pleasure of watching your own blooms, landscaping with native plants over time can give you a backyard view of small native wildlife. More than hummingbird feeders filled with sugar water, more than nest boxes and birdhouses, your most important investment in attracting birds and other creatures is by planting assorted flowering natives to provide several food sources — nectar, foliage, seeds — as well as protective cover and nesting sites.

If you live in a high-country rural area, bushes of Apache plume can provide browsing for deer. Mourning doves will eat seeds from prickly

poppies and beeplants. If you want multi-tasking desert trees that supply food, cover, and shelter for various bird species, you might plant paloverdes, desert willows, mesquites, Mexican elderberries, and saguaros. Despite their barbs and thorns, even chollas and yuccas harbor certain birds that fail to nest elsewhere. Anyone who has had the pleasure of watching an oriole family's nest slung from a yucca will be grateful for such a site in his own yard.

Besides the many indigenous birds you can enjoy regularly, Arizona also draws migrating hummingbirds, flycatchers, and trogons from Mexico. Southeastern Arizona's canyons are the only locales north of the border where some of these tropical and subtropical species roost.

Fortunately, several hummingbird species roam across the state beyond those canyons. The Arizona-Sonora Desert Museum outside Tucson features a hummingbird plant demonstration garden to help you envision such a garden of your own. A desert hummingbird garden might include ocotillo, gilia, sotol, and chuparosa. If you're planting at higher, cooler elevations above the deserts, you can draw hummingbirds with Rocky Mountain beeplant, skyrocket, wild bergamot, various penstemons, and monkeyflowers.

As you watch for winged color in your garden, don't forget butterflies. Across the desert areas, butterflies seek out the blooms of fairyduster, agaves, paloverdes, desert willow, penstemons, and sages. Many high-country flowers can draw butterflies to a garden; your plantings might include various species of milkweed, columbine, and penstemon, along with sneezeweed and prince's plume, just for a start.

Contacts/Sources

The Arboretum at Flagstaff
4001 S Woody Mountain Road
Flagstaff AZ 86001-8775
(928) 774-1442
www.thearb.org

Arizona Department of Agriculture
Attention: Native Plants
1688 West Adams St.
Phoenix, AZ 85007
(602) 542-6408
www.agriculture.state.az.us/
PSD/nativeplants.htm

Arizona Native Plant Society
P.O. Box 41206, Sun Station
Tucson, AZ 85717
www.aznps.org

Arizona-Sonora Desert Museum
2021 North Kinney Road
Tucson, AZ 85743-8918
(520) 883-2702
www.desertmuseum.org

Boyce Thompson Arboretum State Park
(Boyce Thompson Southwestern Arboretum)
37615 East Highway 60
Superior, AZ 85273-5100
(520) 689-2811
www.pr.state.az.us/parkhtml/
boyce.html

Desert Botanical Garden
1201 North Galvin Parkway
Phoenix, AZ 85008
(480) 941-1225
www.dbg.org

Highlands Center for Natural History
www.highlandscenter.org
339 S. Cortez St., Suite B
Prescott, Arizona 86303
(928) 776-9550
The Center sells a booklet it publishes on wildscaping as a guide for landscape design in central Arizona's highlands, plants for different area environments, and the creation of backyard wildlife habitat. Classes and workshops also available.

Native Seeds/SEARCH
526 North Fourth Ave.
Tucson, AZ 85705-8450
(520) 622-5561
www.nativeseeds.org

Tohono Chul Park
7366 Paseo del Norte
Tucson, AZ 85704
(520) 742-6455
www.tohonochulpark.org

Tucson Botanical Gardens
2150 North Alvernon Way
Tucson, AZ 85712
(520) 326-9686
www.tucsonbotanical.org

University of Arizona Cooperative Extension Program
Forbes 301, P.O. Box 210036
Tucson, AZ 85721-0036
(520) 621-7205
http://cals.arizona.edu/extension/needinfo/plants.html
This program is the outreach arm of the university's College of Agriculture and Life Sciences (CALS) in Tucson, Arizona. County branch offices can offer information on certain topics, including agriculture and horticulture. Some extension offices provide public education through trained volunteers called Master Gardeners; for more information, go to http://cals.arizona.edu/extension/mastergardener/.

Reference Materials

Epple, Anne Orth, *A Field Guide to the Plants of Arizona*. Helena: Falcon Publishing, 1995.

Arizona Native Plant Society, *Desert Wildflowers* pamphlet. Tucson: 1991.

Arizona Native Plant Society, *Desert Butterfly Gardening* pamphlet. Tucson: 1996.

Bowers, Janice Emily, *Flowers and Shrubs of the Mojave Desert*. Tucson: Southwest Parks and Monuments Association, 1999.

Busco, Janice and Nancy R. Morin, *Native Plants for High-Elevation Western Gardens*. Golden, CO: Fulcrum Publishing, in cooperation with The Arboretum at Flagstaff, 2003.

Duffield, Mary Rose and Warren Jones, *Plants for Dry Climates: How to Select, Grow and Enjoy*. Tucson: Fisher Warren Jones Publishing, 1992.

Mazier, Cesar, *The Endicott Wildflower Research Project Report*. Phoenix: Desert Botanical Garden, 1996.

Nokes, Jill, *How to Grow Native Plants of Texas and the Southwest*. Austin: Texas Monthly Press, 1986.

Quinn, Meg, *Wildflowers of the Desert Southwest*. Tucson: Rio Nuevo Publishers, 2000.

Taylor, Ronald J., *Desert Wildflowers of North America*. Missoula: Mountain Press Publishing Company, 1998.

Whitney, Stephen R., *A Field Guide to the Grand Canyon*. Seattle: The Mountaineers, 1996.

ON THE GRAND
CANYON'S NORTH
RIM, ASPENS SHADE
A SUMMER ARRAY OF
DAISYLIKE BEAUTIFUL
FLEABANE.
Paul Gill

8

EDIBLE PETALS
Wildflower Recipes

Many of the same native plants that offer food for birds can also intrigue the human palate. Saguaro fruit and prickly-pear fruits, pads, and jellies demand good prices in gourmet food stores. Mesquite-pod flour is being investigated as a commercial foodstuff; native peoples have already used it for thousands of years. Immature devil's claw pods are pickled and sold. Wild desert chilies demand a good price as a culinary spice. Wolfberries are still harvested for syrup-making by members of the Gila River Indian Community.

While all the food uses of Arizona wildflowers are too many to mention here, this sampler of recipes using flowers can give you a taste at your own table. It is just one more way to bring wildflowers into our lives.

Without thinking much about it, we regularly consume flowers: The familiar flowers of artichokes, broccoli, and cauliflower can be found on almost every market produce counter. Flowers have always been part of the human diet, although their use has decreased in this century. Advances in food technology have allowed us to be less dependent on seasonally available foods.

When gathering food, past desert dwellers studied plant flowering patterns and handed the lore down to the next generation. If not to be eaten themselves, flowers were a welcome signal of the coming edible fruits.

Flowers and flower buds serve different culinary purposes. Some can be used as a substantial part of a meal, while others do better as a colorful, distinctive garnish. The recipes that follow are modern adaptations to the ways in which Indians used Arizona flowers in the past. The flowers discussed have been carefully selected and are safe to eat, but not all wildflowers are edible; some, like sacred datura, are poisonous.

You can easily grow in your garden all of the wildflowers recommended for use here. If you collect flowers (or other plant parts) from property other than your own, you must have permission from the owner, otherwise collecting the flowers is illegal. (See Chapter 2.) Illegal flower collecting detracts from other people's enjoyment and limits a plant population's reproductive potential. Plus, by growing and tending your own plants, you can be more confident that they are free from environmental contaminants.

A RIOT OF CHUPAROSA
SHRUBS BLOOM NEAR
THE KOFA MOUNTAINS.
Robert G. McDonald

(All recipes were originally prepared by Ruth Greenhouse of the Desert Botanical Garden.)

Edible Desert Flowers:
Gathering and Preparation

1. Harvest only flowers that have not been contaminated by sprayed chemicals or roadside pollution residue. If you're unsure, don't use them.
2. Collect flowers immediately after they open in the early morning, if possible. Shake off any ants or other insects while outside.
3. Wash thoroughly but gently in cool water.
4. Drain and store between layers of paper towels to absorb excess moisture.
5. Refrigerate until used.

Drying

1. Line a cookie sheet with paper towels or brown paper.
2. Spread out clean, whole blossoms in a single layer.
3. Set in a hot, dry place out of direct sunlight, or place in an oven at 150 degrees or less with the oven door slightly open.
4. Store thoroughly dried flowers in a covered container (flowers must be brittle when crushed).

Yucca Flowers

soaptree yucca
Yucca elata

Joshua tree
Yucca brevifolia

Utah yucca
Yucca utahensis

Our Lord's candle
Yucca whipplei

The large, pale green yucca flowers are delicious both raw and cooked. The flowers of the narrow-leaf yuccas (listed at the side) are considered more palatable than the broad-leaf yuccas like banana yucca. Look for the blossoms from late April until late May. Unless you are going to crystallize the whole blossom as a garnish, only the petals should be used as the flower centers are bitter and a little tough.

Fresh yucca petals, crisp in texture and delicate in flavor, are tasty combined with tender greens in a tossed salad with a vinaigrette dressing. Yucca petals steamed or sauteed until tender, about 10 minutes, taste somewhat like celery and make a good side dish.

Dried yucca petals can be ground into flour and added to soups or stews. The thoroughly dried petals are easily pulverized with a small mortar and pestle. This flower "flour" can be stored in a covered container for future use.

*Egg white (pasteurized), beaten until slightly frothy

Small, soft brush

Fresh yucca blossoms, cleaned and dried

Finely granulated sugar

Crystallized Yucca Flowers (to decorate cakes and other desserts)

Line a cookie sheet with wax paper. Brush flowers, inside and out, with beaten egg white. Dip flowers into sugar. Place on cookie sheet. Dry in oven at 150 degrees or less with door slightly open. Store in covered container.

*Traditionally, crystallized flower recipes used raw egg whites. This is no longer recommended because of the risk of salmonella poisoning. Pasteurized eggs have been heat processed to kill the salmonella bacteria without cooking the eggs.

4 cups clean yucca petals (approx. 24 blossoms = 1 cup petals)

2 cups chicken broth

1 clove garlic

1 cup plain yogurt

1 cup sour cream

Dill weed

Chilled Yucca Flower Soup

Boil yucca petals in chicken broth for 10 minutes. Cool. Puree in blender with garlic. Add yogurt and sour cream. Whirl just until blended. Chill. Garnish with a sprinkle of dill weed and some fresh yucca petals.

SOAPTREE YUCCA / Robert G. McDonald

Chuparosa Flowers

chuparosa
Justicia californica

The red, tubular flowers of chuparosa add a festive touch to recipes at a time of year when other native flowers generally are not available. Chuparosa, dormant during hot seasons, blooms during the cool weather of fall and winter.

Raw chuparosa flowers are cool and crisp with a cucumber-like flavor. They make an attractive, tasty addition to fresh salads or a garnish for meat, fish, or poultry. Soups, fruits, or vegetables can be topped with a dollop of sour cream and a fresh chuparosa flower.

Chuparosa flowers also are good cooked and can be added to vegetable soups or stews.

Try freezing chuparosa flowers in individual ice cubes for a festive look.

Butter or Bibb lettuce

Grapefruit and orange sections

Clean chuparosa flowers

Saguaro seed or poppy seed dressing

Arizona citrus-chuparosa salad

Arrange citrus sections on lettuce leaf. Top with saguaro seed dressing (recipe follows). Sprinkle with chuparosa flowers.

1/2 cup mayonnaise

2 tablespoons honey

1 tablespoon lemon juice

1 tablespoon saguaro seeds or poppy seeds

Saguaro seed dressing

Mix all ingredients together, and toss with your Arizona citrus-chuparosa salad.

CHUPAROSA / Suzanne Holden

CHUPAROSA / Suzanne Holden

Barrel Cactus Flowers

barrel cactus
Ferocactus wislizenii

The flower buds and colorful yellow and red flowers of barrel cacti can be collected in May through October for use in recipes. Flowers and buds of the compass barrel, *F. acanthodes*, are generally avoided because they are bitter.

BARREL CACTUS / Richard Webb

BARREL CACTUS / Suzanne Holden

3 tablespoons butter

3 tablespoons flour

2 cups chicken broth

2 cups chopped barrel cactus blossoms

1/2 cup chopped onion

1 cup light cream or milk

Barrel Cactus Blossom Soup

Melt butter over medium heat. Stir in flour until smooth. Gradually add chicken broth, stirring constantly. Add remaining ingredients except cream. Simmer 10 minutes, stirring constantly. Add cream or milk. Reheat but do not boil.

Buttered Barrel Cactus Buds

Drop barrel cactus buds in boiling water to cover. Boil until tender, approximately 10 minutes. Drain and serve with butter, freshly ground black pepper, and a wedge of lime.

Jellied Barrel Cactus Flowers

After pouring homemade jelly (any type of fruit) into sterilized jars, push a fresh, clean barrel cactus flower into the center of each jar. The hot jelly sterilizes and preserves the flowers. This is especially good with mesquite or cactus fruit jelly.

Paloverde Flowers

foothills paloverde
Parkinsonia microphylla
blue paloverde
Parkinsonia florida

In April or May, paloverdes decorate the desert with their dense yellow flowers. The foothills paloverde blossoms are creamy yellow, while the blue paloverde blossoms are bright yellow. Delicate and mildly sweet, paloverde flowers should be gathered early in the morning as soon as possible after opening. They can be used fresh, cooked, or as a garnish on salads or soups.

3 cups clean paloverde flowers

1/2 cup water

1/2 cup sugar

2 cups milk

2 tablespoons cornstarch

2 lightly beaten egg yolks or 1 well-beaten egg

2 tablespoons butter or margarine

1/4 teaspoon salt

Paloverde Flower Pudding

Simmer paloverde flowers in water until tender, approximately 10 minutes. Drain well and measure liquid. Add milk to make 1 cup. Puree blossoms in blender. In saucepan, blend sugar, cornstarch, and salt. Add milk and blossoms and cook while stirring over medium heat until thick and bubbly. Cook 2 minutes more, and remove from heat. Stir small amount of hot mixture into beaten egg. Return to hot mixture and cook 2 minutes more. Remove from heat and add butter. Chill in dessert cups. Garnish with fresh paloverde blossoms.

Paloverde Pancakes

Add 1 cup of fresh paloverde flowers to your favorite pancake mix. Prepare and serve as usual.

BLUE PALOVERDE / Suzanne Holden

BLUE PALOVERDE / Suzanne Holden

PALOVERDE / David H. Smith

OCOTILLO / Larry Lindahl

OCOTILLO / Les David Manevitz

Ocotillo Flowers
ocotillo
Fouquieria splendens

The bright scarlet, tubular flowers of the ocotillo occur in dense clusters at the tips of long stems in spring. Ocotillo buds as well as the sweet nectar-containing blossoms and the seeds are edible. Use a small rake or hooked stick to pull down the flexible branches so you can reach the blossoms. The flower clusters break off easily, but beware of the tough thorns on the branches.

2 cucumbers
2 tablespoons sugar
1/4 cup white wine vinegar
1/4 cup minced ocotillo buds
2 tablespoons minced parsley
Salt and pepper to taste

Cucumber-Ocotillo Salad
Slice cucumbers into thin slices. Add minced ocotillo buds and parsley. Add sugar and vinegar and toss. Chill 1 hour. Season with salt and pepper to taste.

1 quart ocotillo blossoms
1 quart very warm (not hot) water
2 quarts 7-Up
1 pint vanilla ice cream

Ocotillo Flower Punch
Soak ocotillo blossoms in warm water overnight. Strain and chill; discard the used blossoms. Mix ocotillo "tea" with chilled 7-Up. Add scoops of ice cream. Sprinkle with fresh ocotillo blossoms.

GLOSSARY

ANNUAL: plant that lives, flowers, and dies in a single season.

ANTHER: part of the stamen that produces pollen.

AREOLE: on a cactus, the junction of two or more central spines.

BAJADA: broad desert foothills formed by merging alluvial fans along the edge of a desert valley.

BANNER: upper petal in flowers of the Pea Family.

BASAL: at or near a plant's base.

BIENNIAL: plant that lives and dies in a two-year span, flowering and fruiting in its second year.

BRACT: modified leaf growing at the base of a flower or fruit.

CALYX: outer layer of modified leaves, or sepals, that cover a developing flower bud.

CAPSULE: dry fruit with several divided seed compartments that split lengthwise.

CHAPARRAL: plant zone of dense evergreen thickets, usually of shrubby evergreen oaks.

COMPOSITE FLOWER: a member of the Sunflower Family, having both ray and disk flowers in the flower head.

COMPOUND: leaf that is divided into two or more leaflets.

CONE: dry, woody fruit with overlapping scales.

CONIFER: cone-bearing, evergreen tree or shrub with needles instead of leaves.

COROLLA: as a group, all of a flower's petals.

DECIDUOUS a plant that drops it leaves seasonally.

DISK FLOWER: small, tubular flower, often clustered in the center of a composite flower.

DISSECTED: finely cut or split into many narrow divisions.

FILAMENT: a stamen's thin stalk supporting the anther.

MEXICAN GOLDPOPPIES
MIX WITH FALSE BABY
STARS. David H. Smith

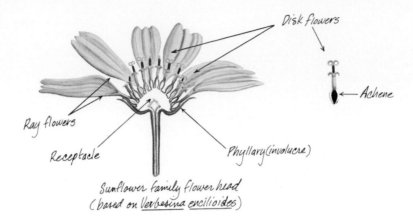

Disk flowers

Achene

Ray flowers

Receptacle

Phyllary (involucre)

Sunflower family flower head
(based on *Verbesina encilioides*)

HERB: nonwoody perennial

INFLORESCENCE: flowers grouped on a stem, such as a panicle or raceme.

INVOLUCRE: distinct ring of bracts surrounding a group of flowers (such as a composite flower).

LINEAR: long narrow shape (such as a leaf) with parallel edges.

LOBE: leaf or petal segment split from the main structure by an indentation.

MONSOON: Arizona's summer rainy season where high temperatures, high winds, and high moisture produce dramatic thunderstorms.

OVARY: at the pistil's base, this part of the flower female organ ripens into a fruit if pollinated.

OVULE: contents of a flower's ovary.

PALMATE: lobed to resemble fingers on a hand.

PANICLE: flower spike with a center stem and smaller branching stems supporting the flowers.

PERENNIAL: plant that lives several years, usually longer than two.

PHYLLARY: in the Sunflower Family, one of the bracts at the base of the flower head.

PINNATE: compound leaf composed of single leaflets set in pairs along a stem.

PISTIL: flower's female reproductive organ, made up of a stigma, style, and ovary.

PROSTRATE: lying flat on the ground.

RACEME: flowers clustered along a single, unbranching stalk.

RAY FLOWER: the outer, straplike flowers that ring the centers of composite flowerheads, often mistakenly called petals.

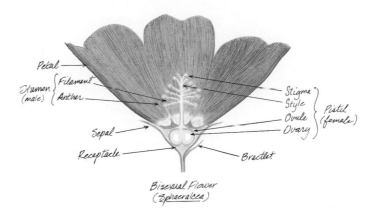

Petal
Stamen (male) { Filament Anther
Stigma
Style
Ovule
Ovary } Pistil (female)
Sepal
Receptacle
Bractlet

Bisexual Flower
(Sphaeralcea)

RECEPTACLE: a flower's axis, or central line, around which the reproductive organs are held.

ROSETTE: circular cluster of leaves fanned around a central point.

SEPAL: individual segment of a flower's calyx.

SEPAL: one part of the flower's calyx.

SHRUB: woody, multi-stemmed plant, usually shorter than a tree.

SPUR: hollow extension on the tip of a flower petal.

STAMEN: plant's male reproductive organ, which includes pollen-producing anther supported by a filament.

STIGMA: part of a flower's female reproductive system, the sticky tip of the style that's fertilized with pollen.

STYLE: stalk supporting a flower's stigma.

SUBSHRUB: perennial with a woody base whose green growth dies back in winter.

SUCCULENT: fleshy plant that stores moisture in its leaves and stems during drought. May also refer to such a plant's tissues.

TAPROOT: large straight root that draws up from deep underground water sources.

TOOTHED: marked by toothlike points along the edge.

TUBER: fleshy underground storage organ that grows from a modified stem or root.

TUBERCLE: stubby or knobby projection on a cactus joint.

VOLUNTEER: seeds and sprouts spontaneously, without being intentionally sown.

COLOR INDEX

RED FLOWERS
barrel cactus, 86
buckhorn cholla, 69
cardinal flower, 89
chuparosa, 35
claretcup hedgehog, 65
climbing snapdragon, 52
coral bean, 84
desert mariposa lily, 45
Engelmann prickly pear, 70
Mexican campion, 94
ocotillo, 50
scarlet cinquefoil, 93
scarlet monkeyflower, 53
skyrocket gilia, 67

YELLOW FLOWERS
badlands mule's ears, 97
barrel cactus, 86
bladderpod mustard, 36
blue paloverde, 70
brittlebush, 32
buckhorn cholla, 69
century plant, 80
cliffrose, 57
common mullein, 96
creosote bush, 36
desert evening primrose, 38
desert marigold, 31
desert mariposa lily, 45
desert prince's plume, 75
desert rosemallow, 87
desert senna, 60
desert sunflower, 50
desert willow, 47
devil's claw, 93
Engelmann prickly pear, 70
fingerleaf gourd, 83
foothills paloverde, 71
golden columbine, 44

golden crownbeard, 61
goldfields, 51
hairy goldenaster, 66
jojoba, 40
mesquite, 71
Mexican goldpoppy, 49
Mojave blazingstar, 37
Mormon tea, 33
orange sneezeweed, 87
purple prickly pear, 54
Rocky Mountain zinnia, 77
skunkbush sumac, 58
yellow monkeyflower, 53
yellow trumpetbush, 76

ORANGE FLOWERS
Arizona caltrop, 88
buckhorn cholla, 69
desert globemallow, 41
firewheel, 34
Mexican goldpoppy, 49
orange sneezeweed, 87
saiya, 81

PINK FLOWERS
brownfoot, 30
California redbud, 46
climbing snapdragon, 52
desert sand verbena, 30
devil's claw, 93
dwarf lousewort, 55
Engelmann hedgehog, 48
Engelmann prickly pear, 70
fairyduster, 31
filaree, 33
fireweed, 84
Goodding's verbena, 34
ironwood, 68
jumping cholla, 92
largeflower onion, 44
manyflowered four o'clock, 54
New Mexican checkermallow, 94
New Mexico locust, 72
owl clover, 46
Parry's penstemon, 55
pincushion cactus, 90

purple mat, 38
Rocky Mountain beeplant, 82
showy milkweed, 81
wild bergamot, 91
wild cotton, 86
Wood's rose, 73
Woodhouse's phlox, 56

BLUE FLOWERS
barestem larkspur, 48
bird-bill dayflower, 83
blue flax, 51
chia, 59
Franciscan bluebells, 90
Mojave lupine, 37
Rocky Mountain iris, 68

WHITE FLOWERS
ajo lily, 35
Apache plume, 49
blazingstar, 37
chaparral fleabane, 66
cliffrose, 57
deer ears, 85
desert chicory, 58
desert willow, 47
fernbush, 82
Joshua tree, 61
largeflower onion, 44
Mexican elderberry, 60
mountain deathcamas, 97
night-blooming cereus, 92
plains blackfoot daisy, 52
prickly poppy, 45
sacred datura, 65
saguaro, 64
Santa Catalina phlox, 56
soaptree yucca, 77
wild cotton, 86

GREEN FLOWERS
canaigre, 40
false hellebore, 95

PURPLE FLOWERS
American speedwell, 76

GENERAL INDEX